✠

JESUS

AND THE

JEWS

✠ ✠ ✠

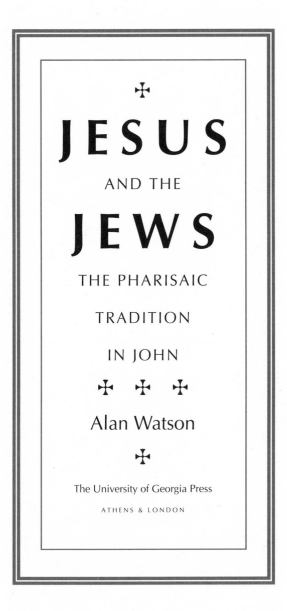

✠

JESUS

AND THE

JEWS

THE PHARISAIC

TRADITION

IN JOHN

✠   ✠   ✠

Alan Watson

✠

The University of Georgia Press

ATHENS & LONDON

© 1995 by the University of Georgia Press
Athens, Georgia 30602
All rights reserved
Designed by Betty Palmer McDaniel
Set in 9.5 on 13 Trump Mediaeval
by Books International
Printed and bound by Thomson-Shore, Inc.
The paper in this book meets the guidelines for permanence and durability of
the Committee on
Production Guidelines for Book Longevity of the
Council on Library Resources.

Printed in the United States of America

99   98   97   96   95   C   5   4   3   2   1

Library of Congress Cataloging in Publication Data

Watson, Alan.
Jesus and the Jews: the Pharisaic tradition in John /
Alan Watson.
p.   cm.
Includes bibliographical references and index.
ISBN 0-8203-1703-9 (alk. paper)
1. Bible. N.T. John—Sources.   2. Jesus Christ—Views
on Jewish law.   3. Law (Theology)—Biblical teaching.
4. Bible. N.T. John—Criticism, interpretation, etc.
5. Pharisees.   6. Jews in the New Testament.   I. Title.
BS2615.2.W38   1995
226.5'06—dc20   94-19437

British Library Cataloging in Publication Data available

For Calum and
Debbie Carmichael

Texts before tosh
—*unattributed*

✝

CONTENTS

✝ ✝ ✝

CONTENTS

CONTENTS

PREFACE

✠ ✠ ✠

THE GERM OF THIS BOOK LIES twenty years back in an interpretation of one episode in the Gospel of John. Very much later I looked to see if my interpretation of that episode had any place in a wider context. This book is the result. So far as I am aware, I had no preconceptions as to what I would find. But we are all conditioned by our history, and I should say something of mine. My introduction to religion was to a severe form of Calvinism which I reacted against from childhood. I wrote my doctoral dissertation on Roman law at Oxford under David Daube, the great authority on biblical law, Mishnah, Talmud, New Testament, and Roman law. Fellow disciples Reuven Yaron and Calum Carmichael have been close friends from my early adulthood. The writings of all three on ancient law, biblical law, Jewish law, and Roman law have been constant companions for more than three decades. The Gospels are replete with law. Because of the above facts, and because by profession I am a comparative legal historian, especially concerned with ancient law, I have often read the Gospels not for theological enlightenment but for legal insights. A particular value for me is that, though the Gospels are not law books, they, and especially John, are concerned to a remarkable degree with "law in action." Roman law studies, and much Biblical study too, concentrate on a search for early developments that have left traces in the product that has reached us. So it can be no surprise that my research on John resulted in a search for one of its sources. This is not a work of faith nor of theology. It is a book by an ancient historian trained to look for and explain inconsistencies within a text and between texts. My main focus is, indeed, on legal history, but the history has implications for religious understanding.

I owe the aphorism "Texts before tosh" immediately to Calum Carmichael, but it goes back to a lesson inculcated by our common master, Daube, who insists that in interpreting a text one must always proceed from the text, not from preconceptions and notions about what must have been. My tool is close textual analysis. John is noted for its realistic details as much as for its ecstatic tone. But theologians concentrate on the latter and St. John's spiritual message. I want to give back the realism to the realistic details.

Because my book deals with what I see as the intersection of early Christian and Jewish traditions about Jesus, and because of tensions and hostilities—to say the least—between Jew and Christian arising from material in the work known as the New Testament, I would like to emphasize that nothing in this book should be taken as indicating my belief in the accuracy of one tradition or another or the veracity of one tradition against another. If a person such as Jesus lived (as I believe), and if he were thought to be a miracle worker (as was commonly supposed), and if he were considered by some as the Messiah or the Son of God, by others not, then evidence would be adduced, often on the same facts, to illustrate that he was or was not. Bad faith, on one side or both, need not be suggested and indeed is not in this book. My concern is not with the historical accuracy of a tradition but with the existence of the tradition.

According to circumstances I have used as a translation from the Greek *The New English Bible, The New Oxford Annotated Bible,* and Brown, *John I–XII* and *John XIII–XXI.* When a translation differs from all of the above, it is my own.

I received a great deal of help and encouragement with this book. All of it, at one stage or another, was read by many friends and colleagues: Sally Curtis AsKew, Calum Carmichael, Steven F.

Friedell, Paul Heald, Olivia Robinson, Tom Schoenbaum, Jim Smith, Frank Stewart, Reuven Yaron. It was also presented to the members of my class on Perspectives in Law at the University of Georgia Law School in the 1993 fall semester. For all their criticisms I am grateful. I am also in debt to Sherri Mauldin, who dealt efficiently and cheerfully with many drafts of each chapter.

But when all is said and done, my greatest debt is to David Daube. It would be ungenerous (and wrong) of me merely to mention that within a week of receiving my typescript, ill and frail as he is, he responded with enthusiasm and with pungent comments on every chapter. Time and again, I find unexpected echoes of his work in my arguments. Without his precept and example I could never have written this book.

✝

JESUS

AND THE

JEWS

✝ ✝ ✝

✠

INTRODUCTION

✠ ✠ ✠

IN THE EARLY SEVENTIES I came to the conclusion that Jesus' encounter with the woman of Samaria had sexual overtones and
that, in fact, she was trying to seduce him. In 1974 in Washington
at a celebration for a friend's legal victory on behalf of Native
Americans, I sought to explain my view with the help of the text. I
could not, because as much as I hunted through Matthew, Mark,
and Luke, I significantly ignored the Gospel of John, where alone
the episode is recounted. I did not associate the elevated and ecstatic John with a rather disreputable story. I returned to the
subject when, reading John Ashton, *Understanding the Fourth
Gospel*, I discovered that my interpretation was novel.[1]

As a consequence, I wrote my 1993 discussion note, "Jesus and
the Woman of Samaria."[2] But I have been uncomfortable since
then, feeling that such an interpretation ought to fit within the
wider framework of the Gospel. Methodologically it was unsatisfactory to treat only one episode. And, indeed, though the basic
idea remains, my understanding of the meaning of Jesus' meeting
with the Samaritan woman has undergone much change.

The present book is a more comprehensive attempt to explain
some of the thrust of John. It is well known that this Gospel is very
different from the other three. The author of John had more than
one source for his materials in a written form or in oral tradition,
and I wished to understand the role of sources that apparently were
not used in the Synoptic Gospels. A number of questions demand
attention. Why is the relatively trivial miracle of turning water

into wine Jesus' first sign, and why does it not appear in the other Gospels? Why are we not told of the immediate response of the guests? Why is the raising of Lazarus, the most striking miracle in the New Testament (apart from the Resurrection), found only in John? Among the episodes common to John and the Synoptic Gospels, but with divergences, one stands out. Why in John is the Crucifixion before the Passover, not after, as in the others?

The answer I eventually seek to establish is that the main source of these episodes, and of some others in John that are told differently in the Synoptic Gospels, is a Jewish anti-Christian tradition. In the environment in which the source was created, Jesus' fame as a miracle worker was too established to be directly challenged. Instead, to discredit him as the Messiah, he was represented as being a rather unsavory individual, hostile to Jewish law and the Pharisees, whose behavior was geared toward insulting or injuring the Jews. An additional, indeed central, aim of the source was to legitimize the Jewish authorities' role in the death of Jesus. Whether the author of John was or was not Jewish (see the closing paragraphs of chapter 10), he also was actively hostile to Jewish religious tradition while accepting as the basic premise that the God of Jesus was the God of the Jews. He seized on the source to establish further signs of Jesus as miracle worker and to represent Jesus as hostile to Jewish rites. He cut out detail inimical to Jesus, but enough remains to provide the picture of the source. Thus, it is not incidental to the story of Jesus and the Samaritan that she says, "What! You, a Jew, ask water from me, a Samaritan woman?" Jesus was about to offend against Jewish tradition because Jews did not use vessels used by Samaritans, and the woman was also to be regarded as unclean. Again, at Cana, turning the water in the purification jars—not other water—into wine served the purpose of preventing its necessary ritual use, and a wedding feast was a religious feast. Again, the episode is shown apart from the reaction of the participants. In the original, some guests would have been shown as far from happy, and John has cut out their reaction. The raising of Lazarus, which never happened (otherwise, it would have figured prominently in the Synoptic Gospels) is deeply dangerous for the Jews. If Jesus could raise from the dead, how could the occupying Roman authorities ever feel secure? What army might he not raise? Retribution would be sure to follow, and the Jews had to be rid of Jesus to save the Temple and the nation. That concern remains prominent in the story and is vital to it in John, though, oddly (if the story were true), the Romans were not in fact worried.

The basic thesis, it should be noted, is intrinsically entirely plausible. The existence among the Jews of a heretical sect—as the Christians would appear to them—would inevitably provoke a reaction, in a tradition to show that Jesus was not the Messiah or the Son of God. This tradition could not always be ignored by Christians who wished to proselytize. To counter it meant dealing with it, and simple contradiction would not do. Rather, episodes in the tradition would be taken, perhaps changed slightly, and their original message blunted. Form criticism allows one at times to discern part of the original message.[3] Robin Lane Fox has recently reminded us, specifically from papyrological evidence in the context of John, that "the Christian scriptures were a battlefield for textual alteration and rewriting in the first hundred years of their life."[4] Yes. And before the scriptures became scriptures, the materials used in them would be subjected to even more alteration. What must be emphasized is that the early tradition about Jesus was by no means unitary. Nothing brings this out more clearly than recent scholarship on Q, a source about Jesus, used by Matthew and Luke but not by Mark, which many would not designate as Christian.[5]

If my thesis is acceptable, we have an advance for Johannine scholarship in general. The circumstances in which John was written, the historical background, the messages to be conveyed, and the audience to be reached should all become clearer.

1
FORM
CRITICISM

☩ ☩ ☩

A WELL-KNOWN FACT about several celebrated works of antiquity is that they are composite in the sense that in whole or in part they derive directly from earlier sources, whether oral or written. Earlier elements are incorporated. This is the case with the epics of Homer—notably, folktales are incorporated in the *Odyssey*,[1] and the famous collections of Roman law, the *Code* and *Digest*, which were made by Byzantine emperor Justinian I. The Hexateuch[2] and the Gospels[3] are also composites. Form criticism, in the widest sense, is the method used to uncover, separate, and explain the various earlier materials. The approach is to look for differences of all kinds between parts of the work. These differences may be contradictions of fact, variations in style, inconsistencies in the use of language, or divergences in human or spiritual values.

My business in this book is with the Gospel of John, but in the first instance I want to approach the issue of form criticism through the medium of Roman law. It is a quirk of scholarship, paralleled in other areas, that form critics, specialists in the Bible, classical literature, or Roman law, seldom take into account the work done by others in their different fields.

Very little of the great works of Roman law has directly survived. By far the largest part of our knowledge comes from Justinian's *Code* and *Digest*. The *Code* (first edition, which has not survived,

4

529; second edition, 534) is a massive collection of written imperial pronouncements, variously called rescripts or constitutions, of previous emperors and of Justinian himself. It is in twelve books divided into titles (or chapters), and each title is devoted to a particular topic, in which the rescripts are set out in chronological order with the name of the emperor or emperors responsible and with the date whenever possible. The task of the compilers was to sift through the vast number of rescripts, discard those that were obsolete, and present those still relevant. In those that still gave the law, repetitions were to be avoided: that is, where two or more rescripts covered the same ground, the compilers had to choose between them. They would also excise passages or whole sections. The compilers were specifically instructed that at appropriate places they were to insert into one rescript something relevant set out in another that was otherwise discarded.[4] That is to say, although the substance in a rescript in the *Code* was found in a written imperial pronouncement, it may not reflect the view of the emperor to whom it is attributed.

The *Digest*, which is twice the length of the *Code*, is a collection of extracts from the writings of the great Roman jurists and is in fifty books, most of which are further subdivided into titles. The original writings run from the first century B.C. through to the end of the classical period, which is traditionally dated to A.D. 235 with the murder of Emperor Alexander Severus. A few texts are from later authors. The compilers of the *Digest* were to reduce the juristic writings to one-twentieth of their original length, cut out all that was obsolete, remove repetitions and contradictions, and not repeat what was recorded elsewhere (that is, in the *Code*).[5] This last instruction is particularly noteworthy. Because the *Code* was prepared before the *Digest*, the instruction means that whenever an imperial rescript simply stated existing law—as most did—then the earlier basis in classical law ought not to appear in the *Digest* (though often, in fact, it does). The compilers were also given power to alter the wording, but not the substance, of the juristic texts. Still, to a much disputed extent, they did alter the substance.[6] For instance, of two forms of classical real security, *pignus* and *fiducia*, one, *fiducia*, was obsolete. If the best account of a rule was stated in the context of *fiducia*, the text might be altered to make it refer to *pignus*.

Within each title, the individual extracts record the name of the original author, the work from which it was taken, and the number of the book in which it appeared: for instance, "Ulpian, *book 22 on the Edict*" or "Papinian, *book 5 of Questions*."

Of course, the compilers did not do a perfect job. For instance, a text originally on *fiducia* but converted rather carelessly to *pignus* might be quite wrong for that form of security. And contradictions remain. Thus, if Africanus gives as the action against the procurator, the general business agent, the action for administering affairs *(actio negotiorum gestorum)*, and the later Ulpian gives the action on the contract of mandate *(actio mandati)*, we may reasonably believe that the texts accurately record the views of the two jurists, that the compilers overlooked the contradiction, and that we have here a historical development during the classical period. An alternative opinion, formerly held by many scholars, was that the classical jurists gave the *actio negotiorum gestorum*, whereas the action in Byzantium was the *actio mandati*; Justinian's compilers changed some classical texts but missed others.[7] Two examples of the complexity of *Digest* texts are set out in chapter 17.

What does this development tell us about the nature of composite works? First, it emphasizes the selectivity of the redactors. John (20.30) has: "Now Jesus did many other signs in the presence of his disciples, which are not written in this book. But these are written so that you may come to believe that Jesus is the Messiah, the Son of God, and that through believing you may have life in his name." Precisely. The selection is not random but purposeful. And the purpose is not to reflect the balance of the original. It is to convey a message to the intended audience. Thus, because of the *Digest* we may know the opinion of the republican Alfenus on some points of the law of sale but not on others. And what we know is not what Alfenus thought was important or was original to him but what the *Digest* compilers thought was relevant and to be communicated to their own and future generations. Again, because the *Code* was published earlier, much law that was established by the jurists does not appear as their work in the *Digest* but is in the *Code* as seemingly the work of a later emperor. Likewise, the choice of subjects in the Gospels reflects not the balance of the sources' interest but the Gospel writer's desire to communicate *his* message to *his* community. Not surprisingly, many Bible scholars believe it is not possible to construct an in-depth biography of Jesus from the Gospels.[8]

Second, the above paragraph alerts us to the difficulties of dating in a composite work. A composite work has more than one source. That a *Digest* text in a particular title gives an opinion of Alfenus is obviously no evidence that the law in the rest of the title is also republican. Conversely, if a rule is first evidenced in the *Code* in a rescript of the emperor Diocletian (284–305), that is no proof in itself that the rule is not earlier and classical. Dating is, of course, easier for the *Digest* and *Code* than for other composite works precisely because each fragment is attributed to a particular jurist or emperor. But it is still not easy. For instance, Ulpian's great commentary on the civil law is entitled *"on Sabinus."* Sabinus lived about two centuries earlier and wrote a short commentary on the civil law, which was Ulpian's model. No fragment of this commentary has survived, but Sabinus is expressly cited by Ulpian, and his views, unacknowledged, will appear in other texts. But the extent of this dependence is impossible to determine. This is so not only for the substance of the law but also for linguistic usage. The frequency of particular words and sentence structures cannot be used to identify Sabinus or Ulpian.[9] Even more, before Ulpian, Pomponius wrote his commentary *"on Sabinus,"* and Ulpian will have made use of it. How much of Pomponius is embedded in Ulpian cannot be known.

For John the obvious point concerns the texts that speak of "the disciple whom Jesus loved" and that are written as if by an eyewitness to Jesus' life.[10] Even if these could confidently be attributed to the Apostle John, the son of Zebedee, we would have no evidence from this for the authorship or dating of the Gospel as a composite. All this must be stressed because even the best scholars, well aware that John is a composite, write at times as if John were a unity.

It may be mentioned in passing that when, as in the *Odyssey* and the Gospels, a particular source is not attributed, it may be very difficult to determine when the use of one source ends and that of another begins.

Third, the compositor is tied to his sources. He may select them as he pleases, cut out elements he does not want, change their emphasis or balance, and even insert small, perhaps important, interpolations, but he does not invent them. They are known not just to him but, at least to a certain extent, to the audience he wants to reach. To be acceptable, the composite must be seen to be a continuation of the tradition. In the nature of things the compositor will leave traces of his work: inconsistencies, inelegant joinings, surprising (in the context) or even shocking assertions, sudden changes of style, even contradictory messages.

Finally, when there is more than one composite work on the same subject, redactors may have chosen to use, or may only have known, different sources. This is true of the *Digest* and *Code* and the Gospels. The results are works that are remarkably different and yet, at the same time, very much the same. We are fortunate when we have such parallel works because they provide vital clues to their sources. With the Gospels we are especially fortunate because Matthew, Mark, and Luke stand together—hence they are called the Synoptic Gospels—and John is much more distant.

I should not be thought to assume that the task of identifying a source used in John is identical to finding interpolations in the *Code* and *Digest*. The sources for the legal works were all in writing; a source in John may have been in writing or been an oral tradition. The emphasis in an oral tradition may be altered more subtly. In the nature of things, legal texts—and hence the sources of a composite work—ought to be clear in meaning, whereas ambiguity may be much more tolerable in theology. A legal text should speak on only one level; a theological text may be multilayered. Apparent disparities in a theological episode may not always be the result of the compositor combining more than one source. Third, the basic source for each legal text is identified, which is not the case in John.

For the relationship between the three Synoptic Gospels, little need be said here. A detailed analysis of the precise use of sources is not needed. It is enough for present purposes to set out in diagrammatic form a general outline that is widely accepted.[11]

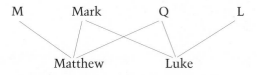

The diagram indicates that the Gospel of Mark was used as a source for both Matthew and Luke (and hence is earlier). So was another source or sources designated as Q—for *Quelle*, the German for "source,"—which was not used by Mark. In addition, Matthew used a source or sources (M) not used by, maybe not known to, Mark or Luke, and Luke used sources (L) not used by Mark and Matthew. The accuracy of the diagram is not my concern. My only purpose is to show the relation of form criticism to composite works in the context of the New Testament.

The chronology of events in Jesus' life is strikingly different between the Synoptic Gospels and John. For the former, Jesus' public ministry was set in rural Galilee with one trip to Jerusalem; for John, Jesus made several visits to the city. The cleansing of the Temple is early in the ministry for John, late for the Synoptics, and a precipitating factor for the Crucifixion. In the Synoptics the Crucifixion comes after the Passover; in John, before. Robert Grant succinctly puts it: "The possibilities, historically speaking, are these: (1) either John or the synoptics, or (2) neither John nor the synoptics."[12] Our main concern at this stage is with textual criticism and now with the relationship of the Synoptics and John. The last word in this chapter may be left to the judicious opinion of Grant:

> There are also many details in which John agrees with the synoptic gospels, and we might suppose that such parallels would clearly indicate John's relative earliness or lateness. Such is not the case. All the evidence is ambiguous, and three possibilities remain open. (1) John did not know either the synoptic traditions or the synoptic gospels, but used independent traditions. (2) John knew some synoptic traditions and used them in his gospel. (3) John knew some or all of the synoptic gospels but consciously rewrote his sources in order to (a) interpret them or (b) supplement them or (c) supplant them. There are no reliable grounds for making a decision.[13]

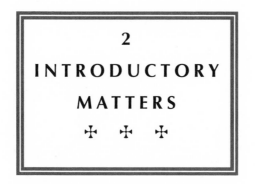

2
INTRODUCTORY
MATTERS
✠ ✠ ✠

I ENDED THE PREVIOUS CHAPTER on rather a gloomy note: that form criticism has not enabled us to determine the relationship between the Synoptic Gospels and John. Still, this does not mean that form criticism will be of no help in establishing the nature of John's sources or the structure of the Gospel. The structure of John has, in fact, been a notorious problem since early times. Suggestions advanced include the notion that the original order was accidentally lost and that sentences, passages, episodes were displaced; that the author combined several independent sources but rather imperfectly; and that the Gospel as we have it is the result of multiple editions.[1]

My ultimate aim is to isolate, examine, and categorize some of the materials used in John, but this cannot, I believe, be achieved directly. Instead, in the first instance I will examine the major episodes that appear in John but not in Matthew, Mark, or Luke: the wedding feast at Cana, the meeting with the Samaritan woman at Jacob's well, the interventions of Nicodemus, and the raising of Lazarus from the dead. To each episode—treating the interventions of Nicodemus as a unit—I will devote an individual chapter. And within each chapter I will draw no argument from the other episodes, though I will not exclude arguments based on other materials. My purpose in this is to avoid reading into one Johannine episode presuppositions drawn from another. To understand the material I will concentrate on the detail, phrase, structure, omissions, and overall emphasis in the episode that seem out of keeping with John's message, the logic of the context, or the thrust of the other Gospels.

Following this I will draw the episodes together in a further chapter for two reasons. First I want to see whether a conclusion reached in one episode helps to render more plausible the interpretation of a different episode. When a structure is as troubling as that of John, it is important to consider links between distinct episodes. Then I want to demonstrate that there is an underlying thrust in the episodes that indicates a common source that can be categorized. This discovery will then enable us to understand better some of the features of the Johannine episodes. The source of the four episodes I will for convenience term S (for "source"), not because it would (necessarily) be the main source for John (if it existed) but because knowledge of it will provide a key to other problems about sources.

For instance, if these four episodes have no common source but rather a variety of sources, then we may have no information as to the knowledge of these sources by the other Gospel authors. From any such source a Gospel writer might have used some other material but not the episode found only in John. But if these four episodes are connected through S, then we can say that S was not used by Mark, Q, M, Matthew, L, or Luke. If S had been used, it would be remarkable, for example, that no one records the raising of Lazarus, the most important miracle. This means that when an episode occurs in John and in at least one Synoptic Gospel, the source for it in the Synoptic Gospel is not S.

This, in turn, may enable further advances. Thus, if an episode occurs in John and in a Synoptic Gospel, the source for John may be S. This becomes significant if the account in John has a different thrust from that of the other(s). If this thrust in John corresponds to that discovered for S, then we can plausibly suggest that it may derive from S about which we now have further information.[2]

As I suggested in chapter 1, the selection of material in a composite work is not random but purposeful, and the purpose is to convey a message to the intended audience. This has been recognized for the Gospels and particularly for John. I accept the common view that the Gospels tell us more about the church situation in which they were written than about the life of Jesus, and I especially admire the formulation of Raymond E. Brown:

> Wellhausen and Bultmann were pioneers in insisting that the Gospels tell us primarily about the church situation in which they were written, and only secondarily about the situation of Jesus which *prima facie* they describe. I would prefer to rephrase that insight as follows. *Primarily*, the Gospels tell us how an evangelist conceived of and presented Jesus to a Christian community in the last third of the first century, a presentation that indirectly gives us an insight into that community's life at the time when the Gospel was written. *Secondarily*, through source analysis, the Gospels reveal something about the pre-Gospel history of the evangelist's christological views; indirectly, they also reveal something about the community's history earlier in the century, especially if the sources the evangelist used had already been part of the community's heritage. *Thirdly*, the Gospels offer limited means for reconstructing the ministry and message of the historical Jesus.[3]

Indeed, the Gospels are the best source of information about the church situation in which they were written and the community's earlier history. Nonetheless, for methodological reasons set out in chapter 10, I will not discuss that church situation in this book.

For my purposes, it is irrelevant whether Jesus was a historical figure or not, though the historical record from outside the canon of the Christian church is strong that he was.[4] What is important is that this record and that for the succeeding century be examined to see what non-Christians thought about Jesus and Christian communities around the time that the Gospels were written and the preceding tradition formed. For present purposes the significant matter is not whether such views were accurate, but simply that they were held, because they may illuminate the source we are trying to isolate. This historical record comprises both Roman and Jewish sources, and we will look at the former first.

Cornelius Tacitus, the historian born around A.D. 50 who perhaps was still writing in 115,[5] records in his *Annales* 15.44:

> Therefore, to suppress this rumor, Nero supplied scapegoats and tortured with the most exquisite punishments those whom the vulgar called Christians and who were hated for their depravity. The founder of this group, Christ, had been executed in the reign of Tiberius by the procurator, Pontius Pilate. The deadly superstition was repressed for the time being, but broke out afresh, not only through Judea, the birthplace of this evil but even in the city [Rome] where all disgusting and shameful practices collect and flourish on all sides.

The context is the fire of Rome of A.D. 64, which Nero was rumored to have instigated. The most significant point in the text is that as early as the sixties of the first century Christians were hated, regarded as a group apart, and considered capable of all wickedness and depravity.[6]

Suetonius, who was born around A.D. 69 and is last recorded in 121/2,[7] states in his life of Claudius, 25.4: "He expelled from Rome the Jews who under the incitement of Chrest [*impulsore Chresto*] continually rioted." "Chrestus" is presumably "Christus." Tertullian, *Apologeticus*, 3.5, reports that Roman rulers mispronounced "Christianus" as "Chrestianus," and Suetonius's statement about the expulsion is in accord with Acts 18.2: "There [Corinth] he fell in with a Jew named Aquila, a native of Pontus, and his wife, Priscilla; he had recently arrived from Italy because Claudius had issued an edict that all Jews should leave Rome." Claudius was emperor from 41 to 54, so even before Nero Christians were regarded as continual troublemakers. The edict applied to Jews generally, though the wrongdoers were those influenced by Christ. The implication is that the Roman authorities did not distinguish. The Jews thus had reason to hate the Christians for whose faults they were punished. That Christ is called the *impulsor*, "instigator," of the riots does not necessarily suggest that Suetonius thought he was present at Rome.

From a letter of Pliny the Younger, 10.96, when he was governor of Bithynia (111–13), and from the emperor Trajan's reply, 10.97, we learn that professing Christianity had been a crime for some time but that Christians were not then actively sought out.[8] Pliny believed Christians to be numerous, considered their religion a depraved and excessive superstition, and reported that they met before dawn on a certain day "to sing a hymn to Christ as if to a god."

But by far the most important text for us—if it is genuine—is from the Jewish writer Josephus in his *Jewish Antiquities*, 18.63f., a work published in 93/94.[9]

About this time there lived Jesus, a wise man, if indeed one ought to call him a man, for he was a doer of marvelous feats, a teacher of such people as receive the truth with pleasure. He drew over to him many Jews and many Greeks. He was the Messiah. 64. When Pilate, upon hearing him accused by men of the highest standing among us, had condemned him to be crucified, those that loved him at the first did not give up this affection for him. For on the third day he appeared to them alive again, for the divine prophets had prophesied these and ten thousand other wonderful things about him. And the tribe of the Christians, so-called after him, has still not disappeared to this day.

But the passage cannot be as Josephus wrote it, and it has been suspected of interpolation since the sixteenth century. Josephus was a

Pharisee and would not have called Jesus χριςτὸς, "the Messiah."
Moreover, the Christian writer Origen, who lived from around 185
to 255, expressly states twice that Josephus did not believe in Jesus
as the Christ.[10] Yet the passage is in all the manuscripts and was
known to Eusebius around 324.[11] Further, the style seems to be
very much that of Josephus,[12] and there is a subsequent passage,
Jewish Antiquities, 20.200, that seems to imply that Jesus had already been introduced to the reader, which would not be the case if
our passage had not existed: "And so he [Ananas] convened the
judges of the Sanhedrin and brought before them a man named
James, the brother of Jesus who was called the Christ, and some
others." Accordingly, though some scholars delete the passage
altogether,[13] it is generally believed that most of the text is genuine.[14] The standard reconstruction is:

> About this time there lived Jesus, a wise man for he was a
> doer of marvelous feats, a teacher of such men as receive the
> truth with pleasure. He drew over to him many Jews and
> many Greeks. When Pilate, upon hearing him accused by men
> of the highest standing among us, had condemned him to be
> crucified, those that loved him at the first did not give up their
> affection for him. And the tribe of the Christians, so-called
> after him, has still not disappeared to this day.

If the text so reconstructed gives Josephus's substance, then we
have textual evidence outside the Bible for a matter that will be of
importance to us, namely, that many Jews who were not persuaded
that Jesus was the Messiah nonetheless regarded him as a miracle
worker. Even without the text we can be reasonably sure that Jesus
was so regarded. Miracle workers, after all, were well known.[15] And
the Gospels are replete with evidence of Jews observing Jesus work
miracles but not being convinced of his divine or messianic stature.
That, indeed, is one of the Gospels' main themes.

Miracle workers were, I have said, well known. Yes, indeed. We
must not forget that the Roman Vespasian, under whom the

Temple at Jerusalem was destroyed in A.D. 70, was in Alexandria in 69, shortly after he was acclaimed emperor by his troops. As he sat on the tribunal two poor men, one lame, the other blind, approached together, entreating to be cured. The god Serapis, they said, had promised they would be cured if Vespasian spat in the blind man's eyes and touched the lame man's leg with his heel. Vespasian hesitated, friends encouraged him, and before a large audience he successfully performed the miracles.[16] Tacitus even writes of "many miracles" occurring in Alexandria at the time, showing the favor of the gods to Vespasian. Thus, the emperor who destroyed the Jewish nation performed publicly two miracles akin to Jesus' greatest.

3

THE WEDDING FEAST AT CANA

✠　✠　✠

FOR JOHN, JESUS' TURNING THE WATER into wine at Cana in Galilee was the first miracle or "sign by which Jesus revealed his glory" (2.11). For modern scholars, it is the most puzzling. John Ashton is led to say:

> Tramping the foothills of biblical scholarship, the exegete is often tempted to stray from the beaten track, and nowhere more so than in the course of investigating the marriage-feast of Cana, where one can easily find oneself waist-high in bracken. The episode is crammed with teasing little problems. What was Jesus' mother (never named Mary in the Gospel) doing at the wedding in the first place? Was it because, as one tradition held, she was the groom's aunt? Or had the whole family recently moved house from Nazareth to Cana? Who invited Jesus and his disciples to the wedding? Was it perhaps Nathaniel, who, we are told in a later chapter (21:2), came from Cana? And at what stage in the celebrations did they turn up? Maybe towards the end of the week, when the wine might well have already been finished, unless it had run out— an alternative explanation—because of gatecrashers to the party. Why did Jesus' mother become involved, and why was

she especially concerned by the shortage of wine? Was only a portion of the water in the jars changed, or was it all turned into wine to ensure a plentiful supply during the celebrations; and how many gallons are there in a firkin anyway? What eventually became of the bride and groom? One medieval tradition makes the groom forsake his bride on their wedding night, leaving the marriage unconsummated, in order to follow Jesus: his name was John, and he was later to write a Gospel! And if none of these questions is easy to answer or indeed seems particularly relevant, then one can lope off instead on a hunt of parallels: Jesus goes one better than Moses, who merely turns the water in the stonejars of the Egyptians (Exod. 7:19) into blood! Even Raymond Brown, who is especially good on this passage, feels free to follow Bernard and others in indulging in such harmless little *divertissements.* There are, however, some serious obstacles to a proper understanding of the passage, this time blocking the main track: they concern the meaning of Jesus' reply to his mother, τί εμοι καὶ σοί, γύναι (v. 4) and of the following sentence (statement or question?) concerning Jesus' "hour." Above all there is the problem of the *significance* of the miracle, whose very singularity (there is nothing quite like it elsewhere in the Gospels) renders interpretation particularly hazardous.[1]

But the episode is even more puzzling than has been suggested. This is the first miracle, but it is essentially trivial. What sort of message was Jesus trying to send that "led his disciples to believe in him" (2.11)? What was Mary's point when she said, "Wine they have not"? What, above all, as we shall see, would have been the reaction by the other guests, about which we are told nothing? Still, the most puzzling fact of all is that there are so many puzzles.

The wedding was on the third day, presumably the third day after the last mentioned episode, the recruitment of disciples who went to see where Jesus was staying and "spent the rest of the day with him. It was then about four in the afternoon" (1.39). Stated times in John are usually significant,[2] and Raymond Brown suggests that the day was Friday, the eve of the Sabbath, hence the disciples would have to stay with Jesus until Saturday evening when the Sabbath was over. On this basis, Andrew would have gone to find his brother, Simon Peter (1.40–42), on Sunday. "The next day Jesus decided to leave for Galilee" (1.43) would be Monday, and he would arrive in Cana on Tuesday evening or Wednesday morning.[3] The Mishnah Ketuboth 1.1 declared that the wedding of a virgin should take place on a Wednesday; hence, if the reconstruction of the timing is correct, Jesus was present from the beginning of the festivities, which has often been doubted. Wedding festivities were expected to last a week.[4]

The Greek makes a distinction between the presence at the wedding of Mary, the mother of Jesus, and of Jesus and his disciples: literally, "the mother of Jesus was there; and both Jesus and his disciples were invited to the wedding" (2.2). In the Authorized Version the distinction is marked by making the presence of Mary verse 2 and the invitation of Jesus and his disciples verse 3. Mary's presence seems more a matter of course, and there is the apocryphal tradition that Mary was the aunt of the bridegroom.[5] For Ashton, "It is to be noted first of all that she was present at the wedding from the start, unlike Jesus and his disciples who arrived later, as invited guests, from the outside."[6] Anyway, when the wine ran out, Mary said to Jesus, "Wine they have not" (2.3).

This remark is open to several interpretations. It may be a simple observation of fact. For some scholars it is a request to Jesus for decisive action, for a miracle.[7] For others, it is a rebuke to Jesus either that he and his disciples had drunk too much or had not contributed to the festivities.[8] Yet again, it may have been a hint, none too delicate, that it was time for Jesus and his disciples to leave. I find rather paradoxical the view of C. H. Dodd that the "general presupposition of the story is that Jesus was a person likely to contribute to the success of a convivial occasion" and that the colloquy between Jesus and his mother has the "suggestion of a certain tension within the family."[9]

Jesus' response is a vigorous protest: "What to me and to you, woman? My hour has not yet come" (2.4). "Woman" is a surprising designation, despite the numerous claims that it is not a rebuke, nor impolite, nor an indication of lack of affection.[10] Certainly, Jesus' normal mode of address to a woman is simply "Woman,"[11] but here he is addressing his mother! There seems to be no parallel to such a mode of address in Hebrew or Greek unless perhaps in John 19.26–27. "Jesus saw his mother, with the disciple whom he loved standing beside her. 27 He said to her, 'Woman, there is your son'; and to the disciple 'There is your mother'; and from that moment the disciple took her into his home." In this context, the dying Jesus could not have addressed Mary as "Mother," since the whole point is that he wanted John to take over the role of son. The address "Woman" is indeed used for distancing Jesus from Mary, a fact that would lend support to the idea of a similar distancing at the wedding feast. Besides, γυνή is by no means Jesus' universal address to a woman. When the woman who had been hemorrhaging for twelve years touched his garment because she thought she would so be cured, he addressed her as "daughter" (θύγατερ) (Matthew 9.22; Luke 8.48). But how much closer ought Mary to have been to him!

"What to me and to you" is a Semitism and, as Raymond Brown emphasizes,[12] has two shades of meaning in the Old Testament. First, it may be used when one person is unjustly bothering another, meaning, "What have I done to you that you should do this to me?"[13] Second, when someone is asked to get involved in something he regards as no business of his, he may respond, "That is your business. How am I involved?"[14] The first, but not the second, implies hostility. If we link "My hour has not yet come" with the preceding sentence (which is uncertain), then his "What to me and to you" has the first sense and is hostile. In any event, Jesus' response indicates he is not taking Mary's remark as simply a casual observation. J.-P. Michaud points out that "What to me and to you?" in a positive context can scarcely be understood as a reply to Mary's demand, and yet it remains negative in its general tenor.[15]

Indeed, to say that "What to me and to you?" in Greek is negative in its general tenor is an understatement. In Mark 1.24 the man with the unclean spirit called out, "What to me and to you, Jesus of Nazareth? Have you come to destroy us?" Jesus rebuked the evil spirit, "Be silent, and come out of him!" (Mark 1.25). Similarly, the man with the unclean spirit who lived and howled among the tombs said, "What to me and to you, Jesus, Son of the Most High God? I adjure you by God, do not torment me!" (Mark 5.7). In Matthew 8.29, this is the wording of the demons cast out into the Gadarene swine: "What to me and to you, Son of God? Have you come here to torment us before the time?"[16] Significantly, it also appears in the Septuagint version of 1 Kings 17.18. God told Elijah that an impoverished widow at Zarephath was commanded to feed him, and she did (1 Kings 17.8ff.). Then her son became deathly ill. She addressed Elijah: "What to me and to you, O man of God?" This is very hostile, as, indeed, appears from the standard translations.[17] It should be noted that when a word or phrase is adopted by one language from another, it does not necessarily have the same range of meaning in its new home that it originally had. The evidence indicates that "What to me and to you" in Greek was predominantly hostile.

To understand the Greek, it is important to note that "τί εμοι και σοί, γύναι" is a Semitism. But it does not follow that the original source was written in Aramaic. Many modern American Jews—and non-Jews, too—who know no Yiddish use an English that is sprinkled with Yiddish words and turns of phrase, as an unnoticed consequence of linguistic tradition.[18] It has been noted that in John Semitisms occur more frequently in dialogue than in narrative. The same is true of modern novels set on American college campuses. But we are not to suppose that the fictional professors are Yiddish scholars or that they spoke Yiddish that has been translated by the novelists or that the novelists have English as a second language or even that they know Yiddish.[19]

The "teasing little problems" now multiply. Mary's response to Jesus' outburst is to tell the servants, "Do whatever he tells you" (2.5). This is entirely inappropriate. Jesus has emphatically told her that the absence of wine is not his business, but she expects him to do something. How, moreover, could she expect him to perform a miracle, because for John the turning of the water into wine was the first sign? Yet few would disagree with Raymond E. Brown that "Mary seems to have no doubt that Jesus will intervene and is uncertain only about the manner of intervention."[20] Incidentally, Mary's command to the servants indicates that she is at the feast in a special capacity. It is important to notice the detail. Mary is at the feast in an honored capacity, and her position there has been distinguished from that of Jesus and his disciples. To this detail I will return in a moment.

Jesus does intervene and turns water into wine (2.6–8). This is the crucial part of the episode but has, I fear, been sadly misunderstood. A proper understanding of this goes far to explain other "teasing little problems." Jesus' response to Mary's instructions to the servants is hostile and violent in the extreme and is full of anger toward his mother. Mary wants wine for the feast, so she will have it! And that to the tune of between 727 and 1090 standard modern bottles of 75cl each. It is a call to drunken excess. Though wine is frequently praised in the Bible,[21] Jewish tradition is hostile to drunkenness.[22] In the Old Testament drunkenness is a precursor to disaster. For example, Noah became drunk, and Ham uncovered his nakedness;[23] Lot became drunk and had sex with both his daughters.[24] In Judith 13.2–8, Holofernes was dead drunk, and Judith decapitated him. In 1 Maccabees 16.15–16, Simon and his two sons while drunk were treacherously slain by Ptolemy, who had hosted the banquet for them. (It has been suggested to me that it is not providing wine but the recipients' behavior that causes drunkenness, and that if I buy a gallon of Scotch on a

Monday, I do not necessarily intend to drink it all that evening. True, but this wine is provided at a feast; it is open wine that will not keep. The point of the story is the sheer extravagance.)

If the wine had run out late in the feasting, a minimum of 727 bottles would be an enormous amount; if early, it would still be excessive.[25] The Gospels do not lead us to believe that Jesus and Mary moved in very wealthy circles where guests at a wedding feast would be especially numerous.[26] But Jesus' excessive response to a delicate situation was the smaller of his offenses at the wedding feast.

For the miracle, the water used was that in the six stone purification jars, each holding twenty or thirty gallons, that Jesus had filled to the brim. On a minor level this seems inconvenient and unnecessary. This new wine would have to be removed from the jar into jugs for distribution. Why not simply have the jugs filled, which would also avoid the problem of excess? On an important level Jesus has obstructed the purification rituals for which water, not wine, was needed.[27]

Purification by water is obligatory under Jewish law.[28] Because a wedding was a religious occasion, this purification would be especially important. John mentions that the jars were of stone. This may simply be factual: stone vessels did not pass on ritual impurity whereas those made of earthenware could,[29] so they were particularly appropriate for ritual use. Or John may be stressing purification. In any event, Jesus has created a serious problem for religious, law-abiding guests at the wedding. Purification by washing the hands with water was needed before breaking bread and before eating any wet fruit.[30] Jesus has obstructed this ritual purification. Since he had no need to use the purification jars in this way, it is hard to believe that he was not deliberately offending against the law.

I should like to pause at this stage and offer my scenario for the events to this point. Mary was present at a wedding, probably as a relative, to which Jesus and his disciples were also invited. For some reason the wine ran out, a fact that Mary pointed out to Jesus, perhaps as a rebuke, perhaps as a request for him to do something. Mary's remark angered Jesus, who said that the lack of wine had nothing to do with him, either in the sense that he had not had more than his fair share or that there was nothing he was going to do about it. Mary persisted and, ignoring his outburst, told the servants to do as he instructed them. She put the onus of acting onto Jesus. This willfulness infuriated Jesus, and in retaliation, "to serve her right," he provided not a reasonable but an excessive amount of wine, while at the same time making the feast unpleasant for many of the guests. He ruined the celebration. Jesus appears as a miracle worker, but as a very human one and one who has no patience for Jewish ritual. In large measure, he acted in order to mortify the honored guest, his mother. This explains the stress on the detail that her position at the feast was different from his. He also wanted to call attention to himself: this is, after all, his first sign. Above all, he is showing contempt for Jewish traditional values.

I should like to emphasize a detail: "Jesus said to them, 'Fill the jars with water.' And they filled them up to the brim" (2.7). This should, in the first instance, put paid to any argument that Jesus did not turn all of the water in the jars into wine but only that which was drawn off. If the water was turned into wine only when it was drawn off, there would have been no need to fill the jars to the brim. In the second place, the point of the detail is to show Jesus' excess just as we are told the number and capacity of the jars.[31]

I am very much aware that readers will be distressed at my interpretation. Again I find Raymond Brown's commentary illuminating:

Theological themes and innuendo so dominate the Cana narrative that it is very difficult to reconstruct a convincing picture of what is thought to have happened and the motivation of the dramatis personae. Some commentators would relieve us of this burden by denying that there is any basic traditional story of Jesus behind the account and by regarding the whole as a purely theological creation. Of course, for those who deny the possibility of the miraculous, all the miracle stories concerning Jesus are suspect. But why is the Cana story more suspect than others?[32]

But the interpretation I have proposed is not theological but a picture of what was supposed to have happened. I believe that (to this point) I have dealt with all the factual issues that arise and have explained all the germane "teasing little problems," apart from Jesus' response, "My hour has not yet come." Many scholars, I think it germane to suggest, have a particular, usually unexpressed, problem with John and his sources. John has a very marked theological vision, and it is often felt—even when not said—that the sources of John have been changed so much that we can never hope to regain a picture of them. In contrast, I would hold that the factual episodes in themselves—if not in their arrangement—contain much of what was in the sources used by John.

But now we should return to the narrative. Jesus ordered the servants to draw off some of the wine in the jars and to take it to the steward of the feast. The steward tasted the wine, was unaware of its source, and saluted the bridegroom: "Everyone serves the best wine first, and waits until the guests have drunk freely before serving the poorer sort; but you have kept the best wine till now" (2.10). End of story. But there is a deafening silence. The steward did not know where the wine came from, nor did the bridegroom, nor did the guests. Sooner rather than later, a guest would want to purify himself/herself with water. But there was no water in the jars. Who would be blamed? The bridegroom, inevitably. Trauma at the wedding feast! Arguments from silence are notoriously dangerous, but a silence in the tradition on this point is unthinkable. From whatever original source was used, the reaction of the guests has been excised.[33] No doubt they could find other water that was not impure, such as from the source for filling the jars, but the very presence of the jars indicates that to use them for purification was more convenient.

It is here that form criticism comes into play and shows its worth. The interpretation I have proposed seems simple, free from problems, and follows naturally from the details of the story. But it is contrary to what appears to be the general tenor of John. I suggest that in the culture in which the author of John lived there was a source, written or oral, that portrayed Jesus as, indeed, a miracle worker, but with very human weaknesses, who exercised his talents in a trivial way, who was not the Messiah, and who was very hostile to Jewish law. John used this episode, but modified it in keeping with the message he wanted to convey. Thus he inserted the spirituality of "My hour has not yet come," and he deleted the reaction of guests to the absence of water from the purification jars. And he added at the end of the episode (2.11) that the disciples believed in him. This source shines through in the details of the original, as is often the case with a composite work. It can be further categorized as Jewish and anti-Christian.

(David Daube also sees in this episode an earlier version utilized by John. He rightly says that "his artificial pattern clearly presupposes a simpler one." But his interpretation is different from mine. He believes that for John, the miracle was not in providing the company with wine where there had been only water but in providing superior wine. He writes, "Surely, the original story culminated in a sentence like: 'And the water was made wine and they gave it to the guests and they found it very good.'")[34]

I have emphasized that this first miracle in John is trivial. It is also commonplace, even though, as Ashton said, "there is nothing quite like it elsewhere in the Gospels." Turning water into wine was a miracle well known to pagan religion and was a miracle associated with Dionysius, the discoverer of the vine.[35] Archaeological evidence attests the feat in Dionysiac worship at a temple in Corinth. As Barrett puts it, "There was thus an exact precedent for the benefaction of Jesus in a pagan worship doubtless known to some at least of John's readers."[36]

Finally, in this chapter I want to call attention to a very different interpretation. Duncan Derrett has stressed the amount of law in the New Testament.[37] He sees this episode at Cana as involving the reciprocal obligations of gifts that have been so well elucidated by Marcel Mauss.[38] The wedding invitation to Jesus and his disciples— his family, in effect—put Jesus under an obligation to make a gift.[39] To fulfill this obligation Jesus presented the bridegroom with the wine. Derrett does convincingly show from the sources that an obligation of reciprocity did exist, was measured and regulated. But that element does not explain the episode at Cana for three reasons. First, an essential element of making such a present was that it be made publicly.[40] In John, the absence of publicity in Jesus' behavior is stressed. Second, reciprocity of gifts demands that the gifts bear the appropriate equilibrium; otherwise, a further gift is required from the recipient. But the amount of Jesus' wine is out of all proportion to the value of the invitation to him and his disciples. Third, Mary's intervention was operative, but it would have been quite unnecessary and irrelevant to any gift reciprocity.[41]

4

THE

SAMARITAN

WOMAN

✠ ✠ ✠

JESUS' MEETING WITH THE SAMARITAN WOMAN, recorded in John 4.4–30, seems much more straightforward than the description of the wedding at Cana. Still, when we take the episode at face value we encounter several peculiarities.

Jesus is resting about noon beside Jacob's well, while the disciples have gone to the town to buy food. He is alone. A Samaritan woman comes to draw water. This is surprising because the time to draw water is the early morning and in the cool of the evening,[1] and the timing of the visit to the well is important because it is the occasion for female sociability. As I noted in chapter 3, when a time is mentioned in John, it is usually significant. Still stranger, as commentators stress, there were springs between the woman's town—if it is to be identified, as it usually is, with the modern 'Askar[2]—and the well. "Why," asks Marcus Dods, "should a woman have come so far, passing good sources of water supply?"[3] Jesus asks her for a drink, a perfectly natural request in the context,[4] except that, as we are told, Jews did not drink from the same vessels as Samaritans.[5] She responds, "What! You, a Jew, ask water from me, a Samaritan woman?" Is this response to be seen as expressing surprise or rudeness? Or is it flirtatious, the beginning of a wider conversation?[6] Certainly, Jews did not use vessels used by Samaritans,[7] but Jesus is a thirsty man, and there is no one else to give him water. Moreover, the great majority of Jews were Am-

Haaretz, scarcely observing, and the woman would have no reason for believing that Jesus was otherwise.[8] Jesus replies that if she knew who he was, she would have asked him, and he would have given her living water. What is the Samaritan supposed to make of this? Jesus has no water. What is she supposed to understand by "living water"? Often "living water" is used to mean spring water, usually better tasting than well water.[9] But an offer by Jesus of spring water, rather than well water, makes no sense here, precisely because Jacob's well was a spring.[10] The Samaritan woman has access to her own spring water! Jesus seems to be offering her nothing she does not already have. And the problem remains that he has not the implements to provide her with any water. If we, from our vantage point, interpret "living water" as something like eternal life, how was the Samaritan supposed to know that? Jesus appears to be playing games. After her obvious response, she asks how Jesus can give her living water. He does not answer the question but says he can give her water after which she will never thirst again. The woman's response is still odder: "Sir, give me that water, and then I shall not be thirsty, nor have to come all this way to draw." The reply is nonsensical, if taken at face value. On the wording, the woman understands Jesus as talking quite simply about water.[11] Otherwise, she could not say that she would never again have to come to draw, which shows she is not talking about eternal life. Yet she does not act as if Jesus were behaving like a madman, which would have been reasonable behavior on her part because, in truth, the fact remains that he does not have the means to provide her with water. Moreover, she would still have had to come to the well to draw water—if not for herself to drink, then for her household needs. The issue is acutely brought out by John Ashton:

> It is easy to see that many of Jesus' utterances in the Fourth Gospel have the flavor of a riddle. . . . "If you knew . . . who it is that is saying to you, 'Give me a drink,' you would have

asked him and he would have given you living water" (4:10). Living water—ύδωρ ζων—the first meaning of this phrase is *running* or *flowing* water. How could the Samaritan woman be expected to know that Jesus was going to understand the word literally (*living* water) and apply it to his own revelation?[12]

How indeed? Jesus next asks her to fetch her husband, she replies that she has none, and Jesus acknowledges this. It emerges that the Samaritan has led a less than respectable life, has had five husbands, and is living with a man to whom she is not married. A woman was expected not to marry more than two or three times.[13] A further surprising feature in the text is that the disciples, on their return, are "astonished to find him talking with a woman" (4:27). Why?

I would like to suggest that much light may be cast on the episode in the first instance if we consider Proverbs 5.15–20:

Drink water from your own cistern and running water from your own spring; 16. do not let your well overflow into the road, your runnels of water pour into the street; 17. let them be yours alone, not shared with strangers. 18. Let your fountain, the wife of your youth, be blessed, rejoice in her, a lovely doe, a graceful hind, 19. let her be your companion; you will at all times be bathed in her love, and her love will continually wrap you round. Wherever you turn, she will guide you; when you lie in bed, she will watch over you, and when you wake, she will talk with you. 20. Why, my son, are you wrapped up in the love of an adultress? Why do you embrace a loose woman?

The sexual implications of the passage are well known. "The joys of sex at home with one's own wife are set in contrast with the bitter and disastrous results of loving a 'strange woman,'" says Marvin E. Tate. "The sexual pleasures of a wife are commended in

vv. 18–19," he continues.[14] In the symbolism of verse 15, the words *cistern* (Hebrew, *bor*) and *well* (Hebrew, *beér*)—"metaphors for the lawful wife," according to *The Jerusalem Bible*[15]—refer to her genitalia. Such a verbal usage is common practice and—even in an age that eschews euphemisms—will be found in American novels of the past decade.[16]

If we return now to John, we may suspect a subtext. The woman, perhaps flirtatiously as an opening gambit to more conversation, asks why Jesus requests water from her. Jesus responds by saying he could give her living water. However this may be intended, the woman covertly takes this as a hint of a sexual advance. She takes "living water" in the sense of semen. What liquid could be more alive? She responds: "You have no bucket and this well is too deep," or "You have no dick and this (my) cunt is too deep." The woman uses *well* with the meaning we saw in Proverbs. In a different context, *bucket* might also be used of a vagina, but with respect to the well it means a penis: that enters the well and goes up and down. Sexual innuendo by a willing woman implying that she is too much woman for the male who comes too close is a common come-on trick. We shall see an example from Apuleius later in this chapter. When Jesus says whoever drinks the water that he can give will never thirst again, she demands it. She takes his words as hinting that he will give her such a stupendous orgasm that she will never need sex again. She wants such good sex. It is on this basis that she wants Jesus' "living water" so that she will never need it again. From her very first words she has been testing Jesus out.[17]

Jesus backs off from the direction in which the conversation is going by telling her to fetch her husband. She responds by stating that she has no husband. She is a free agent!

This approach to the episode enables us to go still further. We now see why we are told the woman is not respectable.[18] She goes to the well at an unusual time when other local women would not be there, either because she has been (as many believe) ostracized or (as I believe) in the hope of meeting a man, perhaps indeed a stranger as Jesus is. In fact, she behaves exactly as she should have done if she wished to meet and entice a male stranger. A well beside a roadway at the heat of noon is precisely where and when she could expect to find a stranger relaxing[19] and no local inhabitants. The alternative would have been for her to wait at a crossroads, a favorite spot for prostitutes to find passing clients.[20] But in my view the alternative was out of the question. The woman is not a professional—there is no sign of that in the texts—and at the crossroads there could have been no pretense. Likewise, we understand why the disciples are "astonished" to find Jesus talking with a woman. A woman at that time and place could not possibly be respectable.

We can now begin to answer a question that has troubled commentators: why does the woman go to this well when there are streams between it and her town? There are, I suggest, three reasons. First, the well is beside a highway; therefore, she is more likely to meet a passing stranger. It is precisely because the road is nearby that Jesus stops there. Second, simply because there is running water between her village and the well, the chance of her being caught out by neighbors is diminished. Any woman who ran out of water would go to a nearby stream and not venture so far as the well. Third, Jacob's well was deep, with a shaft of 106 feet.[21] No passing stranger would have the equipment to draw water. With her bucket, the woman of Samaria could be assured that any male stranger would enter into conversation with her.[22]

The preceding paragraph requires expansion or qualification. There is some doubt as to the whereabouts of the town that is called Sychar in almost all of the manuscripts (4.5). No traces of a town with that name have been found in Samaria. The most common view is that it is modern 'Askar, which lies about one mile northeast of the well. Raymond Brown, who actually gives Sheckem as his translation, objects that this site is medieval. Yet he seems more troubled by the fact that if the woman was from

'Askar she had come so far. Shechem was only 250 feet from the well, he says, and if Shechem is the correct reading, "everything fits." But, no, it does not fit. Brown has to admit: "Probably Shechem was only a very small settlement at the time."[23] But "a very small settlement" does not fit John's description of the Sychar as πόλις, a city (4.4, 28, 30), and that "many" of the Samaritans believed because of the saying of the woman (4.39), and "many more" believed because of Jesus' own words. (I do, of course, accept G. E. M. de Ste. Croix's argument that in the New Testament πόλις corresponds more to our notion of a village than to the Greek notion of πόλις.)[24] Sheckem as a city was destroyed in 128 or more probably in 107 B.C. by John Hyrcanus, who ruled the Jews as ethnarch and high priest. If small villages clustered around modern Balâtah,[25] and the woman was from one of these, her distance to Jacob's well would still not be inconsiderable. But even if Sychar were very close, the thrust of the argument in my paragraph would stand. The woman could still hope to meet a stranger resting at the well and avoid seeing neighbors at that time of day. Even if by some unfortunate chance a neighbor appeared, she had lost little. Further activity was needed before there could be a scandal.

My explanation is strengthened by some parallels in Apuleius, *Metamorphoses*, 2.3. Lucius comes upon Fotis cooking and stirring the pot. He says: "O Fotis, how prettily, how merrily you stir the pot, wiggling your hips. What a sweet sauce you prepare. Happy and even blessed would he be whom you permit to dip his finger in." Here *pot* (*ollula*) is used, as was *well*, with the meaning "vagina." The symbolism is the same. Fotis replies: "Leave me, wretch. Go as far as possible away from my fire. For if my tiny fire should blaze forth even a little, you will burn up inside, and no one can put out your heat but I alone who with dainty seasoning know how to shake both pot and bed." Fotis is very willing and, as I have suggested for the Samaritan woman, seeks to entice the male further, suggesting that she is too much for him.

To this point, I have said as little as possible about Jesus' role in all this. But that must now be examined. The woman has widened the conversation by expressing surprise that a Jew would ask a Samaritan for water. There is more to the issue than that Jews do not use vessels that Samaritans have used. David Daube has pointed out with his usual acumen that, for Jews, Samaritan women were to be deemed unclean.[26] A regulation supposedly of A.D. 65 or 66 declared that "the daughters of the Samaritans are menstruants from the cradle,"[27] and this view would have been held by the more rigid for a considerable time before. Moreover, since Samaritan purification rites were different from those of the Jews, strict Jews would regard Samaritan women—and their men through contact with them—as always unclean. Thus, Jesus' offense against rabbinic teaching is even greater. As Daube observed, this explains a detail previously thought inexplicable: after the disciples returned, "the woman put down her water jar and went away to the town" (4.28). John is emphasizing the nature of Jesus' behavior: he will drink again from the unclean vessel.[28] I would add that the detail might also suggest that the woman's need for water from the well was not that urgent in the first place.[29]

At this point we should go back to yet another detail that is overlooked but that cries out for explanation. As they come to Jacob's well, Jesus is tired out by his journey (4.6). But what about his disciples? They go into Sychar to buy food (4.8). How many disciples are there? By my calculations there are at least two from John the Baptist (1.37), plus Peter (1.41f.), plus Philip (1.43), plus Nathaniel (1.45), thus five, but there may be more who are not mentioned. All would have been tired. But five out of six tired men—the sixth being Jesus—set off to Sychar to buy food for lunch for six. Why are so many needed to bargain and to carry back? They aren't. Yet they go. Not one stays to keep Jesus company. Five go off to carry back the lunch pail of six, leaving the master alone.[30] Why? Oddly, Schnackenburg writes that "we must not ask

35

why they all went off together."[31] The easiest answer is that their absence from Jacob's well is necessary for the episode. Again, why? Their absence is not needed if Jesus is going to reveal he is the Messiah. But it is necessary if the Samaritan is going to make sexual advances to Jesus. The presence of third parties, I suppose, would have been a deterrent.[32]

When the Samaritan expresses surprise that he asks her for water, Jesus replies that if she knew who he was she would have asked him and he would have given her living water. At this stage, she cannot understand Jesus as meaning eternal life, and the meaning, "spring water," which is the obvious, innocent meaning, has to be excluded from her understanding. "Living water" has to suggest something else. Jesus seems to be deliberately encouraging the woman to go further. She does. Jesus leads her on: after the water he can give, she will never want more. After she asks for it, Jesus stops the course of the conversation. She realizes that he is a "prophet." For her then, and for later generations, Jesus' words are understood in their spiritual sense.

Indeed, the whole encounter, as told by John, now takes on a deeper spiritual meaning, as we shall see. Still, the episode reveals a previous layer, an earlier source. For the spiritual point of the story, the woman's sexual advance and Jesus' ambiguous response are quite unnecessary. But they are prominent and must originally have had a purpose. John has not succeeded in removing all traces of the earlier source. I suggest that, in S, Jesus was shown as again offending against Jewish law—indeed, the text emphasizes this directly, by having the Samaritan bring it up. Jesus was also portrayed as less than perfect by his ambiguous response.

But John endows the episode with spirituality. Jesus is shown as dealing with the lowest of the low, a Samaritan, a woman outcast even by her own people, who is even inciting him to sin. He does not condemn or insult her. Rather, he goes along with her, perhaps humors her, and then reveals his true power and nature. She is won over and persuaded, all the more perhaps because of her previous improper conduct. Jesus is to be seen here taking his message at an early point of time to a non-Jew. And he has chosen as the recipient of the news, not the best and most powerful, but the sinner and the powerless.

5

NICODEMUS

✠   ✠   ✠

NICODEMUS APPEARS IN THREE SIGNIFICANT PLACES in John, but he seems rather underestimated by modern commentators.[1] In fact, even in John he is a shadowy figure who weaves in and out. Yet his role is important: he is the instigator of Jesus' first discourse in John (3.1–12); he opposes the arrest of Jesus by the Pharisees before Jesus was heard (7.50f.); and he richly anoints Jesus' body and helps with the burial (19.39–42). He is a more prominent protagonist than any of the disciples. But he appears only in John.

"Nicodemus" is a Greek name not uncommon among Jews in the form "Naqdimon,"[2] and, as Raymond Brown emphasizes, there is no need to regard him as merely symbolic.[3] He was a Pharisee and a member of the Sanhedrin (3.1), the highest Jewish court permitted by the Romans. It is sometimes suggested that his visit to Jesus was not a personal initiative but as a representative of the religious establishment to investigate an unknown, untrained teacher.[4] But there is no indication of that in the text, and in the second and third interventions he appears as distanced from his fellows.

An issue that must concern us, especially because Nicodemus does not appear in the Synoptics, is the relationship between the three interventions. Do they descend from the same source, more than one source, or are these interventions an innovation by John? It seems to me that interventions one and three are thematically linked and illuminate each other, and I will deal with these before tackling intervention two.

Nicodemus comes to Jesus by night. If I am correct that mention of a time in John is significant, then the implication is that he comes furtively, not unreasonable behavior in the circumstances, just as Joseph of Arimathea conceals that he is a disciple "because of fear of the Jews" (19.38).[5] John subsequently stresses this coming by night (19.39). Nicodemus says, "We [plural] know that you are a teacher come from God, for no one can do these signs unless he is from God" (3.2). Presumably these are the signs performed at Jerusalem that are mentioned at 2.23. Jesus' reaction to Nicodemus's faith is hostile.[6] In Raymond Brown's view this is because "Nicodemus's approach to Jesus is well-intentioned but theologically inadequate."[7] Still, hostility toward good intentions seems misdirected. But Jesus' response is not only hostile, it is expressed in a way that is incomprehensible. There is no possibility that Nicodemus could understand "Truly, truly, I say to you that unless one is born from above, he cannot see the kingdom of God" (3.3). I have translated ἄνωθεν as "from above," because that is its meaning for Jesus later in the chapter (3.31).[8] Nicodemus's response shows that he understands ἄνωθεν as "again," which would be, by itself, a perfectly standard meaning of the word in Greek. Brown regards the use of the ambiguous word as part of "the technique of misunderstanding." If this is correct, Jesus' behavior is not geared toward Nicodemus's salvation.[9] Rudolf Bultmann considers the proceedings to be "grotesque."[10] More important for us, the ambiguity and misunderstanding, while perfectly appropriate in Greek, could not have appeared in any appropriate Hebrew word.[11] Thus, the original language for this source of John was Greek, not Aramaic, and here John represents both Jesus and Nicodemus as speaking Greek.[12] Indeed, Nicodemus's misunderstanding is crucial. Accordingly, the whole episode at least as far as 3.11 was composed in Greek.

Jesus continues (3.5–8), and Nicodemus cannot understand: "How can these things come about?" (3.9). Jesus rebukes him, "You are a teacher of Israel, and you do not know these things?" (3.10). Brown considers that the rebuke is because a knowledge of the Old Testament should have given Nicodemus the explanation. But Brown gives no authority for this approach, and I can find none. Bultmann sees in the rebuke a general emphasis on the inability of rabbinic scholarship to provide the answer.[13] I find this suggestion more plausible, but it still does not make the rebuke any more generous in spirit. How was poor Nicodemus meant to know that rabbinic scholarship would not be helpful? It was all he had. Jesus continues his discourse, but Nicodemus has faded from the scene. Indeed, toward the end of 3.11 Jesus switches from addressing him as you singular to you plural.

Thus, in the first episode, Nicodemus visits Jesus, a brave act in itself. He tells him that he recognizes that Jesus is a miracle worker, come from God. Before he gets any further, Jesus responds hostilely, in a way that has to be incomprehensible to Nicodemus and not helpful to him. Nicodemus misunderstands what Jesus is saying, a perfectly natural mistake in the circumstances. Jesus does not set him right but continues his incomprehensible discourse. Nicodemus asks for elucidation and is angrily rebuked. Jesus continues his spiritual discourse as if Nicodemus were no longer there.[14]

In the third episode, Joseph of Arimathea, a secret disciple of Jesus, asks Pontius Pilate for Jesus' body for burial (19.38). "Nicodemus also came, he who came at first to him at night, carrying a mixture of myrrh and aloes of about one hundred pounds" (19.39). They take the body and wrap it with the spices in sheets, as was the Jewish custom, and lay it in an unused grave in a garden near the place of execution (19.40f). We are expressly reminded of the first episode, that Nicodemus had gone to Jesus "at night" (even though he was afraid of his fellow Pharisees). Nicodemus provides a very large and expensive amount of spices for the corpse, about seventy-five pounds in modern measure, fit for a king's burial,[15] an act of supreme charity.

The intervention is deeply moving. Nicodemus, a Pharisee, is distancing himself in the most pointed way from those who wanted Jesus' death. He also dissociates himself forcefully from his colleagues on the Sanhedrin who had brought about the Crucifixion. Yet Jesus had rebuffed him.

But the most important elements in the intervention are those that are not there. As Arthur Conan Doyle put it: "'Is there any point to which you would want to draw my attention?' 'To the curious episode of the dog in the night-time.' 'The dog did nothing in the night-time.' 'That was the curious incident,' remarked Sherlock Holmes."[16]

The first curious element in intervention three is the absence of the disciples, Mary the mother of Jesus, and Mary Magdalene. They should be responsible for the anointing and burial of the body, not the hitherto unmentioned Joseph of Arimathea and the rebuffed Nicodemus. John is making a point about Nicodemus's behavior in contrast to that of the disciples.

A second curious omission is that there is no mention that, by touching the corpse, Nicodemus has made himself ritually unclean for seven days, an important consequence for a Pharisee and member of the Sanhedrin.[17] This ritual uncleanliness must be stressed. Numbers 19.11 lays down: "Those who touch the dead body of any human being shall be unclean seven days."[18] Purification rites were required on the third and seventh day (Numbers 19.12), but the person who touched the corpse was unclean for the whole seven days. Nothing he did could shorten this time. But an unclean person could not celebrate Passover, and for Nicodemus Passover would fall within this period. It was on that account that the Jews would not enter the Roman praetorium when Jesus was taken there: "They themselves did not enter the headquarters, so as to avoid ritual defilement and to be able to eat the Passover" (John 18.28).[19] Nicodemus could eat the Passover a month later,[20] but that is not the same thing at all. Nicodemus has cut himself off from his fellow Pharisees and members of the Sanhedrin for the greatest celebration of the Jewish year, and that to respect the body of Jesus, who slighted him in life and is now defeated in death.

But the most important curious incident in intervention three which did not occur is what links it with intervention one. In intervention one Jesus spoke incomprehensibly about (what Nicodemus understood to be) the necessity of being born again. Jesus has now died and, as we know, will rise again. But not for Nicodemus, to whom, for all Nicodemus's interest in and compassion for him, Jesus was supremely indifferent. The parallel concerns in interventions one and three are life, death, and life after death. Nicodemus does not understand Jesus on being born again, and Jesus does not appear after death, resurrected, to Nicodemus.[21]

If we seek the tradition in the source of these two interventions, we find it has two characteristics. First, Nicodemus is an extremely good and kind man who is very respectful of Jesus. Even when he has been rebuffed, he spends a great deal of money and effort attending to Jesus' corpse, going so far as to make himself unclean for a prolonged time. In contrast, Jesus is portrayed as a rather brutal person, quite indifferent to the feelings of someone even like Nicodemus and unconcerned about Nicodemus's spiritual well-being.

Only a little need be said here about the background to intervention two. The Pharisees and chief priests send officers to arrest Jesus, perhaps for blasphemy (7.32). The officers fail because, they say, "never spoke a man as this one speaks" (7.46). The Pharisees ask if the officers were also deceived and, further, if any of the rulers or Pharisees believe in Jesus (7.47f.). The people who know not the law (that is, the Am-Haaretz) are cursed, say the Pharisees (7.49). Nicodemus, described as he who came at first to Jesus, intervenes (7.50):[22] "Our law does not judge a man before it hears him and knows what he does" (7.51).[23] The Pharisees respond angrily in terms of their well-known antagonism to Galileans:[24] "Surely you are not also from Galilee? Search and you will see that no prophet is to arise from Galilee" (7.52).

As in interventions one and three, Nicodemus is showing extreme generosity of spirit, and his behavior is unexpected, this time quite inappropriate. The Pharisees have not passed judgment on Jesus unheard: rather, they want him arrested and brought in for questioning. The Pharisees curse the common people for not knowing the law, but scholars stress that the Pharisees themselves are showing ignorance of, and disrespect for, the law. Presumably, the law in question is that relating to judging equally and having a full enquiry, which is found in Exodus 21.3; Exodus Rabba 21.3; and Deuteronomy 1.16f., 17.4.[25] But there has been no judgment. Severino Pancaro, whose account of John 7.51 is the most satisfactory and who alone notices that there has been no judgment, cannot quite escape from the traditional exegesis and says: "All that may be said is that such a sentence would be contained *in nuce* in the condemnatory judgment of the Pharisees, voiced in vv. 45ff."[26] These verses give the Pharisees' outraged response to the officers' failure to arrest Jesus, and they scarcely show that they would condemn Jesus without a hearing. Nicodemus's tender feelings for Jesus overcome his intellect.

Intervention two thus portrays Nicodemus in a similar way to interventions one and three. He is much concerned for Jesus and his teaching. Above all, he is a good man.[27] Intervention two need not be taken as coming from a different historical source than interventions one and three.

6

THE

RAISING

OF LAZARUS

✠ ✠ ✠

A FEW HISTORICAL FACTS are requisite.[1] In A.D. 6 the Roman province of Judaea was created out of the annexed territories of Judaea, Samaria, and Idumaea and placed under governors commonly called "procurators." The Jews of the province retained the right to practice Judaism, and this carried with it the privilege of exemption from participation in cults of the emperor. The first Roman administrative act in the new province was a census to assess taxation capabilities. This caused resentment and troubles that were quickly suppressed, but more importantly it gave rise to the nationalist party to whom the only lawful ruler of the Jews was God. The terrorists of this party are believed to have been the nucleus of the Zealots in the rebellion from late 66. Jewish discontent was marked, especially under the procuratorship of Pontius Pilate (26–36/37) (but perhaps only because our evidence is fuller), when we have the first recorded outbreak of terrorism in the province.[2] Even before the creation of the province, messianism had reappeared in a profound way.[3] With the coming of the Messiah, it was believed, the Gentiles would make a final assault upon him, but God would destroy them in vengeance. The messianic kingdom would be set up in the Holy Land, and the dispersed of Israel would return. As we saw in chapter 2, the Jews were expelled from Rome in the reign of Claudius because they continually rioted under the incitement of Christ. The troubles in Judaea became an open rebellion in 66 that was put down by Vespasian (emperor, A.D. 69–79) and his son Titus (emperor, A.D. 79–81). In A.D. 70 Titus destroyed Jerusalem and the Temple. The one episode in the Gospels that we can be most sure did not occur is the raising of Lazarus from the dead. It is by far the most important, detailed miracle. If it had occurred, it would have been deeply embedded in the tradition from the start and, of necessity, would have appeared in all four Gospels. But it is encountered only in John. Raymond Brown has a rather different perspective: "From the contents of the Johannine account, then, there is no conclusive reason for assuming that the skeleton of the story does not stem from early tradition about Jesus. What causes doubt is the importance that John gives to the raising of Lazarus as the cause for Jesus' death. We suggest that here we have another instance of the pedagogical genius of the Fourth Gospel."[4] For me, it is not the subject matter of the Johannine account that proves that it was not part of the early tradition but its absence from the other Gospels, coupled with its overreaching significance. This absence from the Synoptics has, of course, long been noticed by scholars. One common suggestion, rebutted by Brown,[5] is that the story of the raising of Lazarus is a fictional composition based on Synoptic material: it is inspired, it is said, by the story of the raising of the widow's son at Nain (Luke 7.11–16), the characters taken from Luke 10.38–42, and the parable of Lazarus (Luke 16.19–31). But Brown emphasizes that this opinion is based on an approach that has not been successful elsewhere in understanding John, namely, that John is dependent on the Synoptics and does not contain material from a different historical tradition.

It is precisely the importance of the raising of Lazarus for the death of Jesus that persuades me that one can uncover something about this different historical tradition for John. Martha met Jesus and returned home to fetch Mary. There were Jews in the house comforting her, who followed Mary because they thought she was going to the tomb to weep (11.31). They witnessed the resurrection of Lazarus, and many of them came to believe in Jesus (11.45).[6] But some did not, and they told the Pharisees what Jesus had done (11.46). The chief priests and the Pharisees, we are told, called a special meeting of the Sanhedrin (11.47). There is something significantly inaccurate in this because the Pharisees as such had no power to summon the council, though most of the scribes—professional lawyers and one of the three orders of the Sanhedrin—were Pharisees.[7] The elite priests, though, were Sadducees. Brown plausibly suggests that the Sanhedrin would not have moved against Jesus if the Pharisees had not been against him.[8] At the Sanhedrin it was argued, "If we leave him thus alone, all men will believe in him, and the Romans will come and take away both our place (τόπος) and the nation (ἔθνος)" (11.48). Caiaphas, whose intervention causes problems that will shortly be discussed, declared: "You know nothing. Nor do you take into account that it is expedient that one man should die for the people and that the whole nation should not perish" (11.50). This John declares to be a prophesy not only that Jesus should die for the nation but that he would gather together into one the children of God who had been scattered abroad (11.51f.). From that day the Sanhedrin took counsel together to put Jesus to death (11.53).

If some people at the time believed that Jesus had raised Lazarus from the dead, then the Sanhedrin was perfectly justified in its view. The Romans would have, indeed, come and taken away the place—whether τόπος designates Jerusalem or the Temple—and the nation.[9] This was a time of great trouble with the Jews for the Romans. Bar Abbas, who is described as a "notorious prisoner" (Matthew 27.16), was a terrorist (Mark 15.7; Luke 23.19), and so probably were the two brigands or plunders—not simply "thieves"[10]—crucified with Jesus.[11] If Jesus raised one man from the dead, he could raise an army. This miracle was a supreme challenge to the Romans. If Jesus were widely thought to be the Messiah, there would be a full-scale insurrection of the Jews, one that the Romans could not allow the Jews to win. If Jesus were thought to be the Messiah but was not, the result of the insurrection would indeed be to the Jews the loss of the τόπος, the Temple or Jerusalem or both, and the nation. It is entirely in keeping with this that the raising of Lazarus is the last miracle before Jesus is greeted by a large crowd shouting: "Blessed is the one who comes in the name of the Lord—the King of Israel" (12.13).

Verse 48 is, I believe, a clear reminiscence of the fact that in A.D. 70 the Romans did take away the place and the nation from the Jews as a consequence of another religious uprising. It is written with hindsight.

That there could be a genuine fear of an uprising if Jesus were the Messiah must be stressed. Josephus relates that Herod became alarmed that the eloquence of John the Baptist would lead to some form of sedition, so he struck first before the Baptist's preaching could lead to an uprising.[12] John the Baptist stressed that he was not the Messiah,[13] so how much greater would the danger be if Jesus were so regarded?

If we now consider the purpose of the source for John's account of the raising of Lazarus and the reaction of the Sanhedrin up to verse 48, we see that it is to justify fully the role of the Pharisees and the Sanhedrin in bringing about the execution of Jesus. Jesus is for them a very great and pressing danger. Insofar as this source justifies the Sanhedrin and the Pharisees, it is unsympathetic to Christianity.

Though I outlined events up to verse 53, I have omitted from my explanation of the source any mention of 11.49–52. The reason is that I believe that something in these verses comes from a later source, though by basic argument would scarcely be affected if I were wrong. There are various problems. The most obvious is that though John in general appears to have detailed knowledge of Jewish practices,[14] in 11.49 and 11.51 Caiaphas is described as high priest (ενιαυτου), "of that year," as if the high priest were elected for one year only, whereas he traditionally held office for life.[15] As has long been noticed, the author of these verses did not know

Jewish Palestinian practice.[16] Second, Caiaphas begins, "You know nothing," but his stance is precisely the same as that of the others in the preceding verse. The inconsistency is most easily explained as the result of material being excised or of rather carelessly setting together materials from two sources, of which the later might be the author of John himself.[17] As will appear in the following chapter, I prefer the former possibility: the Pharisees opposed Jesus' surrender to the Romans; the Sadducee, Caiaphas, advocated it. Third, 11.51 makes Caiaphas's intervention a prophesy that Jesus would die for the nation, and in 11.52 this is expanded to "not for the nation alone, but also that he might gather into one the children of God who had been scattered." This is a reference to the belief that the Messiah would cause the dispersed Jews to return to Israel, but there is no sign of any such idea in the words attributed to Caiaphas, so it is difficult to see how he could (even unconsciously) have prophesied it.

In this chapter I wish to say little about the miracle and the steps leading up to it. There is clearly a contrast or confusion or conflict between Jesus' love for this family, his unconcern at one stage for their sorrow to come, and his own sorrow subsequently. Elsewhere he shows a reluctance to perform a miracle as a sign; here he allows a situation to develop in order to perform one. Verses 11.5 and 11.6 are mutually inconsistent. More than one source is in evidence.[18]

I said early in the chapter that the raising of Lazarus from the dead did not occur because, if it had, the miracle would be so central that it would appear in all the Gospels. That is only half of the reason. The other half is that if the story had been part of the original tradition the Romans would have been adamant for Jesus' death. In fact, the opposite is the case. The consistent story in John is that the Romans, under the procurator Pontius Pilate, were reluctant to execute Jesus. The priests led Jesus from Caiaphas to the Roman praetorium; they themselves would not go in because they would have become ritually unclean, and they did want to eat the

Passover meal (18.28). Pilate asked what the charge was, and they evaded the question: "If this man had not done evil, we would not have delivered him to you" (18.29f.). Pilate told them to judge Jesus according to their own law. The Jews responded they could not because it was not lawful (i.e., under Roman law) for them to put anyone to death (18.31). After questioning Jesus, Pilate reported, "I find no crime in him" (18.38). Pilate went further, pointing out that it was customary at Passover that he release one prisoner to the Jews, and he suggested he release Jesus (18.39). The offer was refused (18.40). The point for us is simply that the behavior of Pilate is incomprehensible against a background of Jesus' raising the dead. Whatever crime that might be considered to be, a prime necessity for the Romans would have been to repress it. There was, at the time of Pilate's procuratorship, no story of this miracle.

It should be noted that Pilate and the Romans would be forced to act if they knew of the story, even if they did not regard it as plausible. The danger was that some Jews might believe Jesus could raise from the dead and was the Messiah. Then the Jews would rise against the Romans and would, so they believed, destroy them. The Jewish rebellion and victory were central to the messianic message. And messianism was in the air.

7

THE

FOUR

EPISODES

✠ ✠ ✠

SOMEONE WHOSE SOLE ACQUAINTANCE with John was my account of the four episodes would be astonished by the opening paragraph of the first chapter on John in W. D. Davies's brilliant *Invitation to the New Testament* (p. 373):

> In the previous pages we have crossed the rugged plateau of the Synoptic Gospels, the volcanic uplands of Paul and now—to carry the geographic metaphor further—we approach the serene heights of the Fourth Gospel. Sometimes those who have been at home in the Pauline eruptions have not found the serenity of the Fourth Gospel congenial, and the reverse is also true. Archbishop William Temple wrote: "Bishop Gore once said to me that he paid visits to St. John as to a fascinating foreign country, but he came home to St. Paul. With me the precise opposite is true. St. Paul is the exciting, and also rather bewildering, adventure; with St. John I am at home." Perhaps those who have wrestled with moral failure are more at home with Paul, and those who have wrestled with the meaning of the world with John. In any case, to enter John after the Synoptics and Paul is to enter into fresh fields and pastures new.

We have seen nothing of this serenity. Of course, most readers who have come this far will be familiar with the traditional approach to John and will be astonished, even shocked, by my version.

Calum Carmichael, who, so far as I am aware, was once alone in insisting upon a sexual element in Jesus' encounter with the Samaritan woman, is instructive. He rightly observes, "Commentators show a remarkable reluctance to enquire into the male-female aspects of the Samaritan incident."[1] He notes John's fondness for providing realistic detail, and goes on: "Yet in a work so much given to producing higher meanings we should expect this sexual aspect to be explored at another, more elevated level." It is this "more elevated level" of meaning, from episodes in John, that is the focus of attention of Johannine scholars. My approach is different. I fully accept that there are various levels of meaning. I wish to give back the realism to John. I believe I take the episodes at face value with no recourse to symbolism. One of my main propositions for this book is going to be that much of the realistic detail derives not from the evangelist but from a preexisting source, which I designate "S," and is to be explained on a realistic basis. The higher meanings are incorporated by John with remarkable economy. My chapter 16 is devoted to setting out S's realism and John's higher meaning.

I stress the difference in approach because, for me, Carmichael is among the most sophisticated, imaginative, and convincing of the present generation of biblical scholars. For him the episode is not self-explanatory but is to be linked to the preceding debate between John the Baptist and a Jew about purification (3.25ff.): water and purification are prominent in both; Jesus is expressly referred to as a bridegroom in 3.29, and male-female themes are prominent at Jacob's well; at 3.30, John the Baptist says Jesus must increase, and this (Carmichael holds) refers to birth, the consequence of marriage. I try to understand the factual circumstances of the episode in isolation. Though he is well aware that John is a composite, Carmichael treats the realistic details as involved in the spiritual message. I see them as survivors from the preexisting source. On Carmichael's spiritualized approach, the woman could not understand what was going on because a true interpretation, which was meant for later hearers, could only come through linking the episode with John the Baptist's discussion, with which she was not involved. That, I should emphasize, is no barrier to his approach being correct. But aesthetically I prefer to have the woman play out her own agenda. At an earlier stage of my thinking, when I did not link the episode at Jacob's well with a source such as S, I believed Carmichael's approach and mine could be reconciled, only they were at different levels. This belief I now feel is problematic. In keeping with my general practice in this book I will not obscure my narrative with an attempted refutation of a different proposition. Besides, in this case it would be inappropriate. I find no illogicality or inconsistency in Carmichael's approach.[2] Unless my own arguments are inconsistent, the issue is one of plausibility, and that is for others to judge.

Still, to point to the contrast between our approaches, I should like to set out what happens to the realistic details on Carmichael's theory. There is now no significance to Jesus' being left alone at the well. And there is none to the fact that the woman came to draw water at an unusual time. That the woman is to be regarded as unclean now has less importance. Her words, "Sir, you have no bucket, and the well is deep," now have no specific point. That she left her water pot behind is now irrelevant. For me every detail is an integral part of the episode.

That last sentence must be stressed. The strength of my thesis must lie in its power to explain difficulties, and it must rest finally on plausibility. The plausibility depends on my being able to explain *every* realistic detail in an episode involving S, either as coming from S or as a reaction with theological intent against S.

A thesis must always rest on at least one assumption. I want to emphasize my assumption is that realistic details in John have a purpose and are not irrelevant.[3] The resultant thesis from my investigation is that some episodes in John come from a source such as S. My assumption emphatically is not that there was a source, S, with the resultant thesis that realistic details had some meaning.

It is time, however, to look at the four important episodes that occur only in John as a unit to see whether they provide a coherent picture. I believe they do. First, Jesus showed verbal anger beyond all reason to his mother at Cana and to Nicodemus when he came to him at night. He showed himself less than perfect in his indifference to Nicodemus's search for truth on that occasion, in leading the Samaritan woman on, in his pique at Mary, which led him to provide an amazing excess of wine, and in his decision to allow Lazarus to die and be wept over for four days in order that he could be seen to perform a miracle. Jesus appeared actively hostile to Jewish beliefs and practices in needlessly using purification jars at Cana, thus preventing them being used for their ritual purpose, by drinking from the Samaritan's bucket or pot, which was to be deemed unclean, and by in effect notifying Nicodemus at his first intervention that his Jewish faith would not lead him to salvation. Above all, by raising Lazarus from the dead, he placed in obvious and present danger the Temple, Jerusalem, and the whole Jewish nation; this danger was recognized and acted upon by the religious leaders.

This does seem to amount to a coherent picture that demands explanation. My explanation is that these episodes have a common source that was used by John. That source represents Jesus as a miracle worker but one who was not the Messiah. Jesus was by no means perfect: he was a deeply angry man, capable of irrational behavior. He was also actively hostile to, and contemptuous of, Jewish beliefs. In fact, he was such a danger to the Jews that the religious leaders were fully justified in arranging his death.

S was thus a Jewish anti-Christian source, whether written (as I believe) or oral, whose purpose was to show Jesus as an enemy of Judaism, whose execution was necessary for the safety of the nation. It represented Jesus as a miracle worker because the tradition to that effect was too strong to be ignored and because it had to offer plausibility for those hearers who were sympathetic to Christianity. Yet throughout, S, in its anti-Christian stance, was defensive, not aggressive.

On this basis, we can now understand elements in the episodes rather better. First, Jesus responds positively to the Samaritan's advances in the first place, but then withdraws. S has to walk a fine line between portraying Jesus as rather disreputable (which is what is wanted) and being so offensive that the source loses credibility in the eyes of those not positively hostile to Christianity. If Jesus had even touched the Samaritan woman, he would have overstepped the bounds of all decency. Second, we can now see that the role of the Pharisee Nicodemus in S is to be the counterpoint to Jesus. Jesus' failings underscore Nicodemus's goodness. Jesus rebuffs Nicodemus and hostilely refuses to reveal the truth. But far from being offended, Nicodemus seeks to protect Jesus from arrest or judgment. When Jesus is executed, thus appearing to be a failure, Nicodemus exhibits extreme generosity, not only of money but even more of spirit. For S's picture of Nicodemus it is essential that he not be a believer in Jesus. S is Jewish and anti-Christian; Nicodemus is the Pharisee without fault. So, for S, Nicodemus cannot be a Christian. Now we can better understand why the resurrected Jesus did not appear to Nicodemus: for S, Jesus did not resurrect. (This is an appropriate place to stress the importance of tradition in conservative disciplines such as law and religion: it is so powerful that not even John turns Nicodemus into a believer.) Third, at least part of Caiaphas's interjection at the Sanhedrin appears to come from S: "It is expedient for us that one man die for the people and that not all the nation perish." He is stating openly, honestly, and publicly that no legal grounds exist for having Jesus killed but that there is an overriding factor, the safety of the whole people. What has often appeared to be abject cynicism is, in fact, reported as an honorable, decent approach to a heartrending problem: the sacrifice of one individual for the safety of the whole people, when that individual's conduct has created the danger, but not intentionally. It then becomes clear that the view expressed in 11.47f. and in Caiaphas's point at 11.49f. is not wholly self-serving, either for the Sanhedrin or for the individuals.[4]

They faced a dilemma. In the eyes of some or even many Jews, Jesus was a special person deserving protection, but if he were not sacrificed, the whole nation would perish. For the Romans to come and take Jesus would be no solution. Some people would see that as an affront and rebel, thus likewise endangering the nation. The Sanhedrin had to take the initiative in arranging Jesus' destruction.

Caiaphas's interjection is part of a rabbinic development explained by David Daube.[5] What are Jews to do when an enemy force demands the surrender of one of them, under threat of otherwise killing the whole group? The initial stance of the Pharisees was that no one was to be surrendered. That was their position in A.D. 66 when Florus, the Roman procurator, ordered the Jewish leaders in Jerusalem to surrender unidentified individuals who had abused him. This stance became untenable in the persecutions by Hadrian, following the defeat of Bar Kochba in 135. Thereafter, the Pharisees held that a named individual could be surrendered—after all, he presumably had done something to offend—but not an unnamed individual who was to be chosen by the Jews. In our case the Jews are under an occupying power, and they, according to John, have been denied the right to execute a wrongdoer. Among their number is a troublemaker, Jesus, who has committed no crime against the occupying power, the Romans. Still, if he continues in his behavior, an insurrection will break out, and the whole Jewish nation and the Temple will be destroyed. Besides, on many occasions he has publicly, deliberately, and contentiously infringed on Jewish law. The Roman authorities have not demanded his surrender and indeed are most reluctant to get involved. Should the Jews allow matters to take their own inevitably destructive course, or should they get involved and demand that the Romans intervene now and execute Jesus?

The Pharisaic debate became more pointed in the era after 136.[6] But Caiaphas was not a Pharisee but a Sadducee, from a distinguished family, who had been appointed chief priest in A.D. 18 by

Pilate's predecessor, Valerius Gratus.[7] Caiaphas is a collaborator with the Romans—as indicated by his long tenure of office, some eighteen years—as were other Sadducees, in contrast to the more rigid Pharisees. The Sadducees probably had long had a more relaxed attitude on how to deal with a call for surrender of individuals. Daube correctly observes that Caiaphas's angry statement, "You know nothing," shows that he was opposing the original inflexible Pharisaic "no." Daube also points out that it was necessary for the elite Sadducees to co-opt Pharisees on this issue and that throughout history, in times of need, the elite few co-opt numbers.[8] Still, that is not to suggest that here his main concern is not the safety of the Temple and the Jewish nation: the Romans have not demanded Jesus' surrender.[9] Nonetheless, given his high position, Caiaphas cannot be wholly acquitted of looking after his own interests.

(In private correspondence Steven F. Friedell has added a further dimension. He writes:

The story here is reminiscent of the account in B. Talmud, Gittin 55b–56a. The destruction of the Temple was explained as follows. A certain man named Bar Kamza was offended by the rabbis and informed the Roman emperor that the Jews were rebelling. To see if he was telling the truth, the emperor sent an animal for an offering to the Temple, but Bar Kamza made a blemish on the animal, rendering it unfit under Jewish law but not under Roman practice. A dispute arose as to whether to accept the offering so as not to offend and keep peace with the Romans. Another dispute arose as to whether they ought to kill Bar Kamza to prevent him from informing. Rabbi Zechariah ben Abkulas insisted on the strict law on both counts, namely, that the blemished animal could not be offered and that Bar Kamza had not committed a capital offense, and his views were followed. The Talmud's bottom line is given by Rabbi Johanan (third-century Palestine): "Through the humility of Rabbi Zechariah ben Abkulas our House was destroyed, our Temple burnt and we ourselves exiled from our land." Interestingly, Rashi interprets the term *humility* to refer only to the refusal to have Bar Kamza killed. Thus, Caiaphas's position seems similar to the initial position of the unnamed rabbis in the Bar Kamza episode.)

But why, it may be asked, did John make use of S, a tradition that was hostile to his beliefs and message? In the first place, he had no choice. The S tradition was, I suggest, too well known in his time and place. A similar explanation, it should be noted, is often given by scholars to account for the two different creation stories in Genesis 1 and Genesis 2.4–7. Though they were contradictory, each was too well known to be excluded.[10] Secondly, by using S and modifying it to his advantage, he defanged it. He cut out the most hostile implications even in the parts he used. Thus, I suggest, the hostile response of guests at Cana has been excised. Third, like all compilers, John is selective. He has chosen episodes that could be turned to advantage such as further miracles at Cana and the raising of Lazarus. Fourth, S made Jesus very hostile to Jewish law and the Pharisees, and John, who was anti-Jewish, could make use of this emphasis. (I will take this argument further in chapter 15.)

Raymond E. Brown warns in *The Community of the Beloved Disciple* (p. 20):

A further peril in reconstructing community history from the Gospels is to posit nonexistent pre-Gospel sources and to determine the theological outlook of the evangelist (and his community) from the way in which he has corrected the source. In the instance of Matthew and Luke, one has some confidence about corrections of a source, for there is an existing pre-Matthean and pre-Lucan document, namely Mark. But in the instance of Mark and John, pre-Gospel sources are a pure reconstruction, and often one of the criteria for that reconstruction is to place in the source harmonious theological material. In other words, one begins to detect a pattern in what looks like pre-Gospel material, and then one joins other passages to that material on the basis of their being harmonious with it. It is no surprise then that the hypothetical source will emerge with the theological outlook which the exegete used as a criterion in the reconstruction. Admittedly I am oversimplifying here—yet the issue of circular reasoning calls into question judgments about the evangelist's relation to such a reconstructed source.

The warning is apt (and to this quotation I will return in chapter 15). Yet, unless the Fourth Gospel is the work of the son of Zebedee, it must be based on preceding tradition. And in these four episodes we can see a tradition that was not—I will argue—used in the Synoptics. And one can pinpoint some characteristics of this source as I have tried to do. It is a reasonable assumption that S was used elsewhere in John than in these four episodes, in episodes which, in fact, may be paralleled in the Synoptics. But here we must proceed with extreme caution because Brown is only too right about the risks of reading one's own point of view into the texts. One cannot simply proceed by reading John, looking for episodes that seem to have the same thrust as those found for S.

But further progress may be possible on the basis of two questions. First, can a similar thrust to that uncovered for S be found in the Synoptics? If so, this may provide an argument against the hypothesis of S. If not, this will tend to confirm the hypothesis. Second, what differences in treatment are to be found in episodes that appear both in John and in at least one Synoptic gospel?

8

S AND THE SYNOPTIC GOSPELS

✠ ✠ ✠

I HAVE BEEN ARGUING that the four episodes that appear in John but not in the Synoptics have a common source, S, that can, at least to some extent, be categorized. Now we must face the question of whether the qualities discerned for S are paralleled in any of the episodes in the Synoptics. For me the answer is a definite no.

To begin with, there is no equivalent of Nicodemus, the good man, a Pharisee seeking after truth, a nonbelieving protector of Jesus, and a generous spirit. Joseph of Arimathea does not fit the bill. Joseph does request the body of Jesus from Pontius Pilate and arranges for burial,[1] but his standing is very different from that of Nicodemus. He is a disciple, even though a secret one, and there is no hint that Jesus ever rebuffed him.

Even in contrast to the disciples, Nicodemus is unique as the one wholly decent person. Peter is given to anger[2] and denies his association with Jesus three times.[3] John and James, sons of Zebedee, are guilty of the sin of pride,[4] and the disciples are envious and quarrelsome.[5] No figure in the Synoptics can be regarded as a counterpoint to (the imperfect) Jesus as is (the perfect) Nicodemus in John.

Second, there are no episodes in the Synoptics that show Jesus as anything like so ungenerous. Nowhere there does he obfuscate

the issue as he does when Nicodemus comes seeking enlightenment. Also in John he misleads the Samaritan woman and en-
courages her to indiscretion, and this, too, has no equivalent in the
Synoptics.

Third, in the Synoptics, Jesus is not portrayed as exhibiting unjustified anger and resentment toward individuals in the way that
he does toward Mary at Cana and toward Nicodemus when he
comes to Jesus at night.[6] The nearest to it is his diatribe in Luke
11.37ff. against the Pharisees, but the differences must be stressed.
That diatribe is provoked by a specific fact, criticism of Jesus for
not observing Pharisaic rules of religious cleanliness, washing the
hands before eating. The diatribe is not directed against one person
but against the Pharisees in general. Above all, it is an integral part
of Jesus' message. Scrupulosity in observing the trivia of ritualistic
law is misplaced in his view, and what is needed is faith and the
ability to love one's neighbor as oneself.[7] As a Galilean Jew, Jesus
was always likely to be hostile to the Pharisees and their traditions. The clarity of, and justification for, the outburst are in
marked contrast to what we found in John.

Fourth, Jesus' hostility to religious ritual is displayed very differently in John and the Synoptics. In John, at the marriage at Cana,
the turning of the water in the purification jars into wine is a blow
struck against others performing what they regard as obligatory.
Such interference with others' observance of the law does not
appear in the Synoptics. The stress in the Synoptics is always on
what Jesus does on the Sabbath and whether it is justifiable. The
issue may be illuminated by a very different religion, the official
state religion in pagan Rome.

Macrobius, who was active probably in the late fourth or early
fifth century A.D., reports:

> *Saturnalia* 1.16.9 The priests declared that religious holidays
> were profaned if someone worked after they had been pro-
> claimed and prescribed. Moreover, it was not permitted for

the *rex sacrorum* or the *flamines* to see work being done during religious holidays. Thus, they had announced by means of the public crier that people had to abstain from work and any who neglected the order were fined. In addition to the fine, it was maintained that whoever carelessly did any work on such days had to give a pig as a sin offering. The pontiff Scaevola insisted that no expiation was possible for one who acted knowingly. But Umbro said that no pollution was contracted by one who did something pertinent to the gods or on account of religion or regarding the urgent utility of life. Then Scaevola, when he had been consulted on what it was lawful to do on holidays, replied, "Anything whose omission would be harmful." Therefore, if an ox fell into a deep hole and the head of the household set him loose, with the help of his workers, he would not be seen to have profaned the holiday. Nor would one who, when the tree beam of his roof broke, preserved it by a support from imminent collapse.

When the pontiffs declared a *feriae*, a public religious holiday, no work was to be done on it. This was the general rule. But issues of interpretation arose. One question was whether there was a difference in fault according to whether the perpetrator acted ignorantly, carelessly, or deliberately against religion. Another question related to work that could be performed without wrongdoing. In this, there was a difference of opinion. For Umbro, there was no pollution if what was done was pertinent to the gods or on account of religious rites or concerned "the urgent utility of life." Scaevola, *pontifex*, who may be Publius Mucius Scaevola, *pontifex maximus*, chief priest, who died about 115 B.C., or more likely his son, Quintus Mucius Scaevola, *pontifex maximus*, who died in 82 B.C.,[8] took a broader view. For him, anything could be done whose omission would be harmful."[9]

For the Jews, the Pentateuch banned work on the Sabbath but provided little detail.[10] The interpretation of these prohibitions was the subject of enormous rabbinic debate, and in the Mishnah it occupies two tractates, Shabbath and Erabin. Shabbath 7.2 sets out thirty-nine categories of work, including reaping and carrying anything from one place to another. The editor of the Mishnah is always considered to be Rabbi Judah the Patriarch, who was born in A.D. 135.[11] The Mishnah, however, includes a great many provisions from much earlier times, and a large number could have no practical effect after the destruction of the Temple in A.D. 70. On many matters it contains differing opinions by different Pharisaic rabbis, and we can be sure that in the time of Jesus various interpretations might be professed, not all of which have survived.

Two specific examples are enough to set out the problem and highlight Jesus' behavior.[12] Jesus was rebuked by the Pharisees because his disciples plucked some ears of grain as they walked through fields on the Sabbath.[13] Jesus defended their behavior on the basis of David eating the bread of the Presence.[14] The Pharisees' objection was based on the extreme interpretation that plucking a few ears was reaping. This seems to have been already the accepted Pharisaic opinion. Philo, who was roughly contemporaneous with Jesus,[15] wrote: "It is not permitted to cut any shoot or branch, or even a leaf, or to pluck any fruit whatsoever."[16] The other instances of Jesus offending the Pharisees because he worked on the Sabbath are all cases when he was doing good to others.[17]

One of these is making the blind man see on the Sabbath, which appears in John 9.1ff. (I am making no claim that the episode appeared in S: see chapter 14). It is recorded in great detail. Jesus "spat on the ground and made mud with the saliva and spread the mud on the man's eyes, saying to him, 'Go, wash in the pool of Siloam'" (9.6ff.). Healing on the Sabbath when the illness was not life threatening was forbidden if it involved working.[18] Kneading is one of the thirty-nine forms of work prohibited by Mishnah Shabbath 7.2. It might be suggested that little hardship would be suffered if Jesus delayed his cure a day or two. But that presupposes their paths would cross.

My point is that consistently in the Synoptics as in John Jesus is shown as strongly opposed to rigid Pharisaic interpretations of the law, especially with regard to the work permitted on the Sabbath. His own stance is made explicit in Luke 14.1ff.:

> On one occasion when Jesus was going to the house of a leader of the Pharisees to eat a meal on the sabbath, they were watching him closely. 2. Just then, in front of him, there was a man who had dropsy. 3. And Jesus asked the lawyers and Pharisees, "Is it lawful to cure people on the sabbath, or not?" 4. But they were silent. So Jesus took him and healed him, and sent him away. 5. Then he said to them, "If one of you has a child or an ox that has fallen into a well, will you not immediately pull it out on a sabbath day?" 6. And they could not reply to this.

This interpretation is reminiscent of that of Quintus Mucius on Roman religious holidays, and it is contrary to that of the Pharisees as represented in John.[19] But nowhere in the Synoptics does Jesus, as he does at the marriage of Cana in John, actually obstruct others in the performance of what they consider to be their religious obligations. (Jesus' question in verse 3, as it stands, is rather unfair. There was nothing unlawful in healing, as such, on the Sabbath. Rather, the prohibition was in working on the Sabbath, and most forms of healing would involve working. At the very least there would be a psychological presumption that an act of healing was working.)

Fifth, the stories of Jesus raising the widow's son at Nain and Jairus's daughter are recorded very differently in the Synoptics from his raising of Nicodemus in John. For the two Synoptic episodes, outstanding features are Jesus' lack of personal involvement with the families of the deceased and the strength and immediacy of his compassion. Jairus asks that Jesus come and lay hands on his daughter so that she will live (Mark 5.22f.). Jairus is then told by others that she is dead (Mark 5.35), and Jesus immediately responds, "Do not fear, only believe" (Mark 5.36). He goes to the house and, despite being ridiculed by others, takes the child by the hand, says, "Little girl, get up," and she is alive again (Mark 5.38ff.). The episode is recounted similarly in Luke 8.41ff., 49ff. At Nain the widow's son is being carried out of the town for burial (Luke 7.11ff.). This time we are given no indication that the widow has faith in Jesus or has even asked him to intervene. Instead, when he sees her, he has compassion and says, "Do not weep" (Luke 7.13). Jesus touches the bier and says, "Young man, I say to you, arise," and he does (Luke 7.14). Usually, being asked to intervene is an important part of the story, one reason being to achieve public effectiveness. In contrast, the story of Lazarus is given great prominence. Jesus is a friend of the family, and he loved Lazarus. But, though he had plenty of notice, he allowed Lazarus to die so that he could perform a sign. He was dilatory in the extreme in raising Lazarus and careless of Mary and Martha's anguish. There is a distasteful element in his attitude quite out of keeping with his behavior at Nain and with the raising of Jairus's daughter. For C. H. Dodd, the delay that allows the illness to reach a fatal conclusion is "a dramatic or picturesque detail."[20] But it is a detail that reflects no credit on Jesus.[21]

Last, as we saw in chapter 6, the Sanhedrin and the Pharisees are represented as justified in desiring the death of Jesus: otherwise, he will be the destroyer of the Temple, of Jerusalem, and of the nation. In contrast, nothing is said in the Synoptics that would in any way justify the behavior of the Pharisees. On the contrary, from the earliest episodes, the Pharisees are out to trap and destroy him, for personal and trivial reasons. In Matthew, the precipitating factor that first causes the Pharisees to take "counsel against him, how to destroy him" (Matthew 12.14) is his curing of the withered hand on the Sabbath. This surely is an extreme and unjustified reaction. The same precipitating factor is found in Mark 3.6. In that Gospel, moreover, a parable against the Pharisees is given as the reason for their wishing to arrest him and to entrap him

(Mark, 12.12f.). Likewise, in Luke 6.11, the curing of the withered hand appears first as the immediate cause of conspiring against him, but even before that they question whether he has committed blasphemy[22]—a crime punishable by stoning to death—for saying, "Man, your sins are forgiven you," when he cures the paralytic (Luke 5.17–26). They also lie in wait for him, to catch him out, because he speaks against them.

The conclusion I wish to draw is that there is nothing in the Synoptics that meshes with the characteristics I have described for a source that was used in John for the four episodes unique to John. Accordingly, I regard this as an indication that I am justified in postulating such a source, S, for John that was not used in the Synoptics.

9

JOHN AND THE SYNOPTIC GOSPELS

✠ ✠ ✠

IN CHAPTER 7 I TRIED TO SHOW that the four major episodes unique to John shared a common source, S, some of whose characteristics could be categorized. In chapter 8 I wanted to demonstrate that with these characteristics S was not a source used in the Synoptic Gospels. In this chapter I will look at episodes that occur in John and the Synoptics, but where the account in John is significantly different. I will argue that features in the versions in John correspond to the characteristics found for S and that, in fact, their treatment has been affected by the use of S. The episodes are the cleansing of the Temple, the Last Supper, the argument made to Pontius Pilate for the execution of Jesus, the arrest itself, and two details in the Crucifixion.

The cleansing of the Temple appears in all three Synoptic Gospels (Matthew 21.12f.; Mark 11.15–17; Luke 19.45f.) with minor variations, but they are very different from John 2.13–17. The main differences are in the timing of the event and in the specificity of the detail.

For the Synoptics, the cleansing occurs at the very end of Jesus' ministry. In Matthew and Luke it is on the day Jesus enters Jerusalem in triumph; in Mark it occurs on the following day. In contrast, in John, Jesus cleans out the Temple at the very begin-

ning of his ministry, immediately after his miracle at the marriage in Cana.[1] In fact, he is not reported as having performed any other miracles at this stage. Only at 2.23 are we told that many believed because they saw the miracles that Jesus was performing in Jerusalem during the Passover.

The timing of the incident has seemed important to many scholars. Despite verbal similarities of the Greek, there is no proof that John used the Synoptics. Nor does it seem to me that one can establish that the authors of John and the Synoptics directly used the same source or sources. What must be certain is that all four Gospels reach back to the same tradition that concerned the same episode. Obviously, we cannot harmonize the Synoptics and John by suggesting there were two cleansings of the Temple, one at the beginning, one at the conclusion, of Jesus' ministry. The question of the timing is therefore much discussed, on the assumption that the event actually took place, but no consensus has been reached.[2] For me, it is irrelevant whether the event actually occurred. What matters is simply the timing of the episode in the tradition that is at the root of the Gospels. One argument, already professed by many scholars, seems to me conclusive for the accuracy of the Synoptics: such a serious affront to worship in the Temple would have forced the priests to take prompt action; hence, it could only have occurred shortly before Jesus' death. Animal sacrifices were very important in the ritual of the Temple and, in fact, were allowed only there and at the Temple of Onias in Leontopolis in Egypt. (In Deuteronomy 12 and 16.5f., worship was centralized—presumably at Jerusalem—and sacrifice was to be offered only in one place. But there were fallings-off. One cause of the ostracism of the Samaritans from other Jews was their worship and sacrifice at Mount Gerizim.) Sacrifices ended in Jerusalem with the destruction of the Temple in A.D. 70. (The Temple of Onias was closed by Vespasian in 73.) In fact, in Matthew (21.15) the chief priests and scribes became angry at Jesus' behavior; in Mark (11.18) and Luke (19.47) it caused the chief priests and the scribes to begin looking for a way to put him to death. A supporting argument for favoring the timing of the Synoptics is that only after having performed many miracles could Jesus have had the authority to act in this way. As we shall see, even in the mildest version the cleansing of the Temple was very much a revolutionary act—at that, a revolution against Judaism, not against the Romans. Throughout the Gospels Jesus is shown as being actively hostile toward the Pharisees, but the main Temple priests were Sadducees. So Jesus' revolutionary action was against both these important wings of Judaism.

But why then is the timing different in John? An answer is best left until we have looked at the specificity of the details. In Matthew 21.12 Jesus "entered the temple and drove out all who were selling and buying in the temple, and he overturned the tables of the money changers and the seats of those who sold doves." Mark 11.15 adds nothing. Luke 19.45 has even less: "Then he entered the temple and began to drive out those who were selling things there." In contrast John 2.14ff. reads:

> In the temple (ιερόν) he found people selling cattle, sheep, and doves, and the money changers seated at their tables. 15. Making a whip of cords, he drove all of them out of the temple, with the sheep and the cattle. He also poured out the coins of the money changers and overturned their tables. 16. He told those who were selling the doves, "Take these things out of here! Stop making my Father's house a marketplace!"

Matthew, Mark, and John mention dove sellers and money changers, though Luke does not. But otherwise Matthew and Mark mention only those buying and selling, whereas Luke refers only to sellers. In John there is no generality: the sellers trade in cattle, sheep, and doves. Only in John (2.15) does Jesus make a whip to drive the sheep and cattle sellers out of the Temple.

The specificity in John has a twofold effect. It makes Jesus' behavior more outrageous—he takes a whip to those he disapproves of and his violence is directed solely against religious practices. The function of the money changers is well known and not what we find at the present day. At that time silver coins were valued by weight. There were only two basic standards, the denarius and the drachma, both acceptable in Jerusalem. The issue was that the Temple tax was not to be paid in coins that portrayed the emperor or had a representation of a pagan deity. Only Tyrian coinage was acceptable. The Temple tax was a half-shekel,[3] which equaled two denarii or a didrachm. The money changers gave those who had to pay the tax half-shekels in return for denarii and didrachms. Presumably, the money changers made some profit on the exchange. Still, the presence of the money changers was expressly permitted and regulated by rabbinic law. Mishnah Shekalim 1.3 declares that the tables of the moneylenders were to be set up on the twenty-fifth day of Adar. Oxen, sheep, and doves—doves for the poor[4]— were the sacrificial animals,[5] and these had to meet strict requirements.[6] The sale of doves in the Temple for sacrifice at any time was under the control of the Temple authorities (Mishnah Shekalim 6.5). There was no prohibition on anyone satisfying his need for a sacrificial beast by buying it in the Temple. Selling cattle there was lawful (Mishnah Shekalim 7.2).[7] Thus, the people driven out of the Temple or otherwise disturbed by Jesus performed a religious or quasi-religious function. At the very least, their presence in the Temple precincts made it easier for others to fulfill their religious obligations. Those referred to nonspecifically in the Synoptics as selling were not selling postcards, curios, or souvenirs; they were directly working in the service of religion. Not only that, but the word I have translated as *temple* is ιερόν, which designates the whole area of the sacred enclosure including the porticos and courtyards. The animals for sacrifice, and therefore their sellers, were in the Temple precincts, not the Temple itself. And the precincts were enormous.[8] On this basis it is not even easy to see why Jesus became so upset. From the standpoint of rabbinic law, Jesus' behavior was incomprehensible, outrageous, and criminal in various respects: assault, disturbance of the peace in the holy place, interference with the collection of the required Temple dues, interference with the required Passover sacrifices. The enormity of Jesus' behavior will be realized when we recall that in Deuteronomy 12, God had centralized worship and sacrifice at one place—for the Jews in Jerusalem, at the Temple. In fact, Jesus' behavior is apocalyptic: he attacks the animals as well as the vendors and overthrows the tables.

C. K. Barrett's commentary is instructive. He believes "the opportunities for buying and selling were not always abused." He then observes that we have little firsthand knowledge of the practices—actually we have none—and concludes that the narrative "may suggest that the proceedings were not entirely unobjectionable."[9] He seems uncomfortable with Jesus' behavior, and his argumentation is weak. There is nothing in the narrative to suggest that Jesus' behavior was caused by wrath at opportunities for buying and selling being abused. In the narrative the anger is directed against the very fact of buying and selling.

Significantly, a writer like W. E. Hull seeks to minimize Jesus' violence. He insists that the whip of cords was not a cruel leather lash—worshippers would not have access to weapons in the Temple precincts—but made of material readily available such as "stalks used either in worship (somewhat like our branches on Palm Sunday) or as food or bedding for the animals."[10] Raymond Brown seems to share this approach.[11] Both ignore the fact that in the precincts would be the whips to drive the oxen and the ropes to tether them.[12] Since Jesus is said to have made a whip, he used the tethering ropes.

Accordingly, I would relate the differences in the account of Jesus cleansing the Temple in John from that in the Synoptics to the influence of S. That portrayed Jesus' act as both uncontrolled and a deliberate affront to standard behavior furthering Jewish ritual and law. The time of the episode was deliberately moved forward: right from the earliest days of his ministry, Jesus was violently hostile to Jewish observance and law, both Sadducee and Pharisee. It is entirely in keeping with this that John (2.18) records that the Jews raised questions about Jesus' authority to act as he had done, but gives no indication of a desire for vengeance. S makes Jesus virulently hostile to the Jewish religious tradition, but plays down any desire of the Sadducees or Pharisees to kill him until he poses a real threat to the Temple and the whole nation. Incidentally, the affront to the Sadducees at the beginning of Jesus' ministry and the role of Caiaphas, the Sadducee, in Jesus' death are among the indications that persuade me, as I claim in chapter 13, that S was a Pharisaic source. For S, Jesus is hostile not only to Pharisaism but to both religious wings of Jewry in Judea, and it is a Sadducee, not a Pharisee, who encompasses his death.

The second episode involves the Last Supper, but only two details, the timing and the Eucharist. I mentioned earlier that when times are given in John they are important. So it was again with the cleansing of the Temple and now with the Last Supper. The point is that in the Synoptics the Crucifixion occurred after the Passover; in John the Crucifixion—and therefore necessarily the Last Supper—happened before the Passover.

In Matthew 26 the Last Supper is portrayed as a Passover meal. The disciples ask Jesus where he would like them to arrange for him to eat his Passover dinner, he gives instructions, and they make preparations (Matthew, 26.17–19). After dinner they sing the Passover hymn and go to the Mount of Olives (Matthew, 26.30). A very similar account is in Mark (14.12–26) and in Luke (22.1–39), who even has Jesus saying: "How I have longed to eat this Passover with you before my death!" (Luke 22.15).

In contrast, in John there is none of this. We are told, "Now before the Passover feast Jesus knew that his hour had come that he must leave this world and go to the Father" (13.1).[13] Then comes the Last Supper (13.2ff.). Jesus is crucified and we are told: "Because it was the eve of Passover, the Jews were anxious that the bodies should not remain on the cross" (19.31). In no way could the Last Supper be a Passover meal in John.

But that the meal was Passover dinner is fundamental for Jesus as Messiah, whose ministry is above all to the Jews. Once more there is a basic problem in timing. Raymond Brown is forced to conclude that "for unknown reasons, on Thursday evening, the 14th of Nisan by the official calendar, the day before Passover, Jesus ate with his disciples a meal that had Passover characteristics."[14] This is most unconvincing. The one Gospel, John, that puts the Last Supper before the Passover has a dinner that has no specifically Passover characteristics. Brown's view would force us to hold that a source of John cut out from the tradition the Passover characteristics of the Last Supper, a source of the Synoptics altered the time of the Last Supper to make it a Passover feast, and Jesus and his disciples ate a last meal that had Passover characteristics but was not Passover, "for unknown reasons." It is much simpler to hold with Joachim Jeremias that the Last Supper was a Passover dinner.[15] Again, the timing in John has been altered. Why? If one accepts the existence of S, there is no problem. The main purpose of the S tradition is to separate Jesus, miracle worker though he is, from the Jews and their religious rituals. For S, and hence for John, he should not be represented as celebrating the Passover.

Some scholars do believe that they see in John 13.21–30 traces of the Last Supper as a Passover meal.[16] This would suit my case that the Last Supper was accurately portrayed in the Synoptics as a Passover meal and that the timing in John 19.31 has been altered because of the use of S, which portrayed the Last Supper otherwise. But the evidence seems to be inconclusive and unpersuasive. The main argument must be that in all four Gospels (Matthew 26.20; Mark 14.18; Luke 22.14; John 13.12, 23, 25, 28) the participants are represented as reclining (ανακείμαι is the verb used), not as sitting. Yet sitting was usual at meals. For Jeremias: "It is *absolutely impossible* that Jesus and his disciples should have *re-clined* at table for their ordinary meals. How is it then that they recline at table in the case of the Last Supper? There can be only one answer: at the Passover meal it was a *ritual duty* to recline at table as a symbol of freedom, also, as it is expressly stated, for 'the poorest man in Israel.'"[17] This goes too far. Reclining was obligatory at a Passover meal,[18] but it was also usual at a party or a feast.[19] Thus, when the woman poured ointment on Jesus' head he was 'reclining' at meat in the house of Simon the leper (Mark 14.3). Likewise, at the house of Levi, Jesus and many tax collectors and sinners reclined at dinner. And the Last Supper was certainly a more important occasion for Jesus than these. No more conclusive is Jeremias's correct observation that in John the Last Supper was eaten in a state of levitical purity (13.10).[20] That was no doubt usual for eating the Passover lamb, but was also usual on other special occasions. More to the point, the rabbinic sources do not support the notion that it was necessary to eat the Passover lamb in a state of levitical purity.[21]

The other detail from the Last Supper is the Eucharist itself. At the end of the meal Jesus took a loaf of bread, broke it, gave it to the disciples, and said, "Take, eat: this is my body."[22] As David Daube insists, if there had been no precedent for this, "his disciples—to put it mildly—would have been perplexed." And he convincingly shows that the precedent was in the Passover liturgy.[23] In the liturgy, prior to the meal a portion of unleavened bread is broken off, taken from the table, and brought back at the end of the meal, to be distributed to the company as the last bit of food that night. Traditionally, this piece of bread is termed *Aphiqoman*. The word is not Semitic but the Greek αφικόμενος or εφικόμενος, and it means "the coming one," or "he that cometh," and represents the Messiah. When Jesus at the finale of the meal breaks bread and says, "Take, eat: this is my body," he is saying to the disciples, "I am the Messiah." The Eucharist appears in Matthew, Mark, and Luke, and it is in the highest degree significant that it is entirely absent from John.[24] For S, the Last Supper must in no way appear as a Passover meal. The detail was not in S, and the redactor has not inserted it. The Eucharist element in the Synoptic Gospels but not in John and its connection with the Aphiqoman is for me the final proof that the Synoptics correctly show the Last Supper as a Passover meal.[25]

We can go further. Eucharistic-like details do appear in John at 6.50–58, in a context that is not Passover or the Last Supper, but in the synagogue at Capernaum (6.59), and in which they do cause confusion and horror or anger. Jesus declared he was the living bread come down from heaven and that the bread he would give for the life of the world was his flesh. "The Jews then disputed among themselves, saying 'How can this man give us his flesh to eat?'" (6.52). Jesus responded, saying *inter alia* that those who ate his flesh and drank his blood might have everlasting life; otherwise, they would have no life in them (6.53ff.). Many of his disciples found this teaching offensive (6.66). As a result: "Because of this many of his disciples turned back and no longer went about with him" (6.60). Thus, Eucharistic-like details outside of Passover in John are both mystifying and horrifying; in the Synoptics in the Last Supper they cause no surprise. The contrast shows that there can be no doubt that at the Last Supper as Passover in the Synoptics Jesus was revealing himself as the Aphiqoman, the Messiah.

One aspect of the Last Supper has given me pause and made me wonder whether it is not, after all, John who has got the timing right. The aspect concerns the nature of the Passover and the time of Jesus' arrest. The Passover celebrates the Israelites' deliverance from the Egyptians. It is a festival celebrating among other things divine and vindictive retribution on a conquering people. "[T]he rite of the blood made it possible to connect the Passover with the story of the killing of the Egyptian firstborn (Exodus 12.23)."[26] In the Synoptics the priests fear to arrest or kill Jesus before or during the Passover because of the anger of the crowd. In John, the arrest and subsequent execution take place before Passover. But it is precisely at Passover that, if Jesus were widely believed to be the Messiah, trouble would erupt. That is exactly when the people would expect—as a parallel with past history—God to reveal himself and destroy their enemies. If Jesus were thought by some to be the Messiah, then the leading priests should act quickly to have him killed before revolution could begin on the Passover. So is John not accurate in staging the Crucifixion before the Passover, before troubles would erupt?

The answer is to be found in another detail where John differs from the Synoptic Gospels. Only in John is Jesus shown as the Messiah whose existence may produce revolution at Passover. Only in John does he raise Lazarus from the dead, causing the reaction of Caiaphas that we have already seen. Only in John is Jesus greeted by a crowd hailing him with "Blessed is the king of Israel" (12.13). There is nothing so strong in Matthew (21.9), Mark (11.10), or even in Luke (19.38), where he is called the "king who comes in the name of the Lord." Thus, in Luke Jesus is hailed as a spiritual king, in John, as the king of the land, an earthly king. It is absolutely necessary for John, but not for the other gospels, that Jesus be executed before Passover. In the Synoptics, only at the Last Supper does Jesus tell his disciples in effect that he is the Messiah. There is a wonderful logical progression in John: from Jesus raising Lazarus, to the meeting of the Jewish leaders and Caiaphas declaring it expedient that one man die for the nation, to Jesus being hailed by the crowd as king of Israel, to Jesus being arrested by Temple police and Roman soldiers before Passover, to Jewish leaders demanding that Pilate execute him, to Jesus being crucified before Passover.

The next episode concerns a detail leading up to the Crucifixion. The Crucifixion and the involvement of Pontius Pilate are in all the Gospels, but this detail is unique to John. The chief priests have turned aside Pilate's request to know what crime Jesus has committed: "If this man were not a criminal, we would not have handed him over to you" (18.30). Despite great pressure, Pilate is most reluctant to act (18.31ff.; 19.1ff.), and Jesus has evaded answering whether he is a king (18.37). Then comes the detail that concerns us (19.12): "From then on Pilate tried to release him, but the Jews cried out, 'If you release this man, you are no friend of the emperor. Everyone who claims to be a king sets himself against the emperor.'" The priests are forcing Pilate to act on his own account and on behalf of Rome.[27] They insist that Jesus is guilty of *maiestas*, treason, against the Roman emperor in claiming to be king. They give Pilate a direct warning: if he releases Jesus, he is no friend of the emperor.[28] This persuades Pilate to act. He presents Jesus to the Jews: "Here is your King" (19.14), "Shall I crucify your King?" (19.15). The chief priests continue the charade as loyal Roman subjects: "We have no King but the Emperor" (19.15). Pilate at procurator had had much trouble with the Jews, had behaved tactlessly at best, was not a success, and after an atrocious episode involving the deaths of many Samaritans was recalled to Rome in 36 or 37.[29] Perhaps our detail is a historical reminiscence: Pilate had to act because he was already in trouble. But our interest is different. We saw in chapter 6 that in John, but only in John, Caiaphas and the chief priests were shown as justified in having Jesus killed to save the Temple and the nation. But now John goes further. The priests are the instigators of Jesus' death, but he is crucified not for an offence against the Jews but by the Romans for a crime against the Romans and, in fact, for the most serious Roman crime of all. This is consistent with the characteristics of S. I said that Pilate was most reluctant to act. So he was, but this reluctance is stressed even more in the Synoptics (Matthew 27.11ff.; Mark 15.1ff.; Luke 23.1ff.). Indeed, in Matthew 27.19, Pilate's wife even intercedes on behalf of Jesus. And in Luke 23.7, Pilate tries to "pass the buck" by sending Jesus off to Herod.[30]

But if Jesus was condemned by the Romans on a Roman charge and executed by the Romans in a Roman form of execution, why, it may be asked, did S involve the Jews at all in the death of Jesus?[31] The answer is the same as I have already given to the question of why John used S. The tradition was simply too strong to be swept aside. Likewise, the blame for playing the leading role in Jesus' death could not be shifted to Pilate. S did the most it could by showing that the Jewish authorities were justified in seeking Jesus' death. Here, moreover, we should go back a little in time. In Matthew 26.47ff., Jesus is arrested by a crowd from the chief priests and elders of the people. In Mark 14.43ff., the arresters were a crowd from the chief priests, the scribes, and the elders. Luke 22.47 mentions only a crowd, but 22.50 has a slave of the high priest in a prominent role, and 22.52 indicates that the chief priests, the officers of the Temple police, and the elders had come for Jesus. John 18.3 stands in sharp contrast to the Synoptics: "So Judas brought a detachment of soldiers together with police from the chief priests and the Pharisees." The word translated as *detachment* in the *New Oxford Annotated Bible* is σπεῖρα, at that time the standard Greek word for the technical Latin *cohors*, a unit of the Roman infantry. At 18.12, their officer is called χλίαρχος, the standard Greek translation of the Roman rank of *tribunus militum*. So only John involves the Roman army in the arrest. To that extent, the role of the Jewish authorities is downgraded. In a similar vein, in John 18, there is no clear indication that Jesus was tried by the Sanhedrin rather than interrogated unofficially by some Jewish leaders. But the accounts in the Synoptics seem to have a trial before the Sanhedrin: Matthew 26.59ff.; Mark 14.53, 55ff.; Luke 22.66ff. In at least Matthew and Mark the trial is fully illegal because the Sanhedrin could not meet at night or outside of the Temple precincts in a private house (Mishnah Sanhedrin 4.1, 11.2), among other reasons.[32] Thus, with regard to the arrest of Jesus and to the treatment of him before he was handed over to Pilate, we can still detect the influence of S.

The first detail of the Crucifixion itself that is indicative of S is a detail of omission in John, but it is nonetheless significant. In all three Synoptic Gospels Jesus on the cross is mocked by the chief priests and the scribes. Thus, Mark 15.29ff. reads:

Those who passed by derided him, shaking their heads and saying, "Aha! You who would destroy the temple and build it in three days, save yourself, and come down from the cross!" In the same way the chief priests, along with the scribes, were also mocking him among themselves, saying, "He saved others; he cannot save himself. Let the Messiah, the King of Israel, come down from the cross now, so that we may see and believe." Those who were crucified with him also taunted him.

Matthew 27.39–44 echoes this account. Luke 23.35–37 mentions only the Jewish leaders, but adds the soldiers to the mockers. In contrast, John mentions no mocking of Jesus on the cross. I believe that in S the dying Jesus was not mocked. S is a Jewish source, hostile to Christianity. It tries to portray the Jews in a favorable way—the behavior of the Pharisee Nicodemus, the priests' full justification for having Jesus put to death—except as they are viewed through the eyes of the hostile and instransigent Jesus. For Jews to mock the dying Jesus—and his death was needed—would be unnecessarily nasty; hence, it had no place in S.

I wish to suggest finally in this chapter that another detail of the Crucifixion, unique to John, derives from S or the tradition of S: the breaking of the legs of the two brigands but not of Jesus (19.31ff.). In my view, David Daube correctly associates the breaking of the legs with the popular Jewish belief that disfigurement might stand in the way of resurrection. This led in the period 100 B.C. to A.D. 100 to various changes in the mode of execution, particularly of stoning, to avoid mutilation. From this perspective, Daube insists that "the anti-Christian party used the disfigurement as an argument against the resurrection of Jesus. John is warding off an attack, he asserts that things did not happen as his opponents imagine and wish them to have happened. That is also why he adds so emphatically that it is his version which gives the truth."[33] John has: "He who saw this has testified so that you also

78

may believe. His testimony is true, and he knows that he tells the truth" (19.35). In S, or at least in the tradition behind S, Jesus' legs were reported to have been broken, and this has been dropped from John, who insists on the contrary, from personal experience. To this subject I will return.

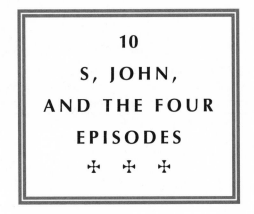

10

S, JOHN, AND THE FOUR EPISODES

✠ ✠ ✠

I HAVE MINIMALIST AIMS in this book, and I should now like to set out what I have not done.

I have not attempted to define the Johannine community or the audience expected to be reached by the redactor.[1] I do accept, as I stated in chapter 1, that a compositor selects his materials for the group he intends to reach, not for their original message. But, with John, if we are trying to elucidate a source, we must not at the same time define the audience. The problem is that we have no system of control. We have no evidence for the specific Johannine community outside of John—even if we believe they were Gnostic in some sense or connected with Qumran—and outside of John we have no evidence for his sources except what was common to the Synoptics (and that is not what I am trying to trace). If we defined the community from the text of John and then used the definition to explicate the sources, we would be arguing in a circle. This would especially be the case because John had more than one source. In so far as the sources were alive in the tradition, he could not altogether reshape or ignore them, even though he could be selective and alter their message. The end result will not fully reflect his intended message. This is very much the case for legal works like Justinian's *Code* and *Digest*, which I discussed in chapter 1.

They tell us relatively little specifically about his Byzantine world. Likewise, the French *code civil* of 1804 is no true reflection of the Napoleonic era.[2] The most that we can do for John is try to isolate details or episodes that seem out of keeping with the overall thrust. Again, I have made no use of linguistic analysis to separate one source from another. The problem this time is that we have absolutely no control. The extremely divergent views on the extent of interpolations in Justinian's *Digest* is indicative of the difficulties that exist when there is no system of control. We do not know how many sources John used or how he used them. For example, did he use only one source for each episode, or did he combine several, or did he select one as his prime source and then insert details from others? And how far did the redactor inject his own words into the Gospel? I do accept that even when there is no control, linguistic analysis may, at times, take us some distance in isolating sources. But in the present context, for my purposes, a search for precision is misplaced. An attempt to be too precise can only result in a loss of accuracy. I could admire, but not make much use of, Rudolf Bultmann, *The Gospel of John: A Commentary* (Philadelphia, 1971).[3]

Nor have I sought to date John, place the gospel in a geographical setting, or rearrange the episodes in what I judge to be their chronological order. Nor have I said anything about his theological message.

This last point brings me to the main theme of this chapter, why John made use of S at all. I have already indicated the answer in chapter 6: S was too well known to be ignored, John could defang it by changing emphasis, he could be selective in his choice of episodes, and in any event S, in representing Jesus as very hostile to Jewish tradition, gave John's own perspective. But now we have to look at the specific episodes from this perspective.

Raymond Brown stresses the richness of theological motifs in the changing of the water into wine at Cana.[4] He points out that the stress in John is not on the replacing of the water with wine, nor on the resulting wine, nor on Mary's intercession and then her persistence, nor on the reaction of the steward or the bridegroom. The primary focus is on Jesus, who will bring salvation to the world. What shines through, Brown says, is Jesus' glory and the belief of his disciples. Cana, he claims, reveals the glory of Jesus by messianic replacement and abundance. This, I believe, is correct. But then it must be emphasized that this primary focus is allowed one verse out of eleven allotted to the episode: "Jesus did this, the first of his signs, in Cana of Galilee, and revealed his glory; and his disciples believed in him" (2.11). Three verses are devoted to Mary's intercession and persistence (2.3ff.) and three to the wine steward (2.8ff.). While keeping a great deal of the episode as it was in S, John has completely changed its meaning. As I argued in chapter 3, he has cut out the hostile reaction of the guests and stated in one short verse at the end the revelation of Jesus' glory and the disciples' belief.

The prime theological message in the meeting of Jesus with the Samaritan woman (4.4ff.) is brought about also with little manipulation of the wording. The behavior of Jesus and the woman is left basically unchanged, but what appeared in S as outrageous behavior for a Jew now comes to represent his taking his message at an early stage of his ministry to non-Jews, even to the despised Samaritans,[5] and among them even to the rejected and sinning. Nothing had to be done to the words *living water* (4.10f.) for a theological meaning to emerge for John's audience.

The first intervention of Nicodemus (3.1ff.) could be used as a peg on which to hang the powerful first discourse about the Son of man. In the process the emphasis shifts from Jesus' ill-treatment of Nicodemus to the theological message. The second intervention (7.50f.) could be retained to show the hypocrisy of the Pharisees' judging Jesus without a hearing. And the third intervention, Nicodemus providing spices for Jesus' burial, contains nothing that is obviously hostile to John's message.

With regard to the raising of Lazarus (11.1ff.) the stress in S would be on Jesus' lack of sympathy for the sufferings of Lazarus, his family, and friends and above all on the fact that because of this act the priests had to have Jesus put to death to save the Temple and the Jewish nation (11.47ff.). Little was needed to put the Johannine focus on Jesus' meeting with Martha and Mary, his sympathy then, and the ensuing, most important miracle. But some indication of his lack of sympathy is still left express! "But some of them said, 'Could not he who opened the eyes of the blind man have kept this man from dying?'" (11.37).[6]

From this perspective, too, we should view the last verse of John: "But there are also many other things that Jesus did; if every one of them were written down I suppose that the world itself could not contain the books that would be written." John admits to being selective. But is there more to it? Is the admission meant to turn aside an attack that he has omitted episodes from S, episodes that could not be so easily laundered?[7]

It is not (yet) my claim that S was the main source of John (though I will argue in chapter 13 that S provided most of the episodes in Jesus' life) or that it was the sole source of John that was not used by the Synoptics. A further detail found in John but not in the Synoptics is illuminating for John. As I have stressed, our knowledge of John's sources is very limited. For the purpose of discussion, but with no particular basis in observable fact, let me postulate that there were four sources, C, K, P, and S.

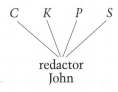

$$C \quad K \quad P \quad S$$

redactor
John

We do not know the relationship between C, K, P, and S. One may be dependent on another; two or more of them may derive from an earlier source. Indeed, before reaching John, S may have been combined with another source and already defanged. But to be used in

John, the sources must all pass through the redactor, whose own original input is also unknown. Now we may move toward the detail that interests us. It is usually believed that John has a great understanding of Jewish tradition.[8] But we have seen one howler in 11.47, where John improperly has the chief priests and the Pharisees call a special meeting of the Sanhedrin. An even bigger gaffe occurs in 11.49, 51 where Caiaphas is described as high priest for that year, whereas the high priest held office for life. The confusion is compounded in 18.12ff. where Annas, Caiaphas's father-in-law, appears as the high priest (18.19) as does Caiaphas himself (18.13, 24).[9] How can John know at the same time so much and so little about Judaism? The answer lies in the nature of compilations. Different sources have different levels of awareness. But who here is ignorant of Jewish tradition? Not S, as we have seen in preceding chapters. Therefore, the events in 18.12ff. have another origin, and not all of the proceedings before the Sanhedrin in 11.47ff. are from S, unless "for that year" in 11.49, 51 is an interpolation (perhaps suggested by 18.13). More important, at least the redactor must be at fault for this blatant mistake. The conclusion must be that however often Jewish ritual is accurately portrayed in John, that understanding is to be attributed to preexisting sources. The redactor, John himself, had little personal knowledge of Judaism. So knowledge of Judaism in the Gospel of John provides no evidence that the author was Jewish or was acquainted with Judaism from within.[10] Ignorance of even one fundamental point indicates that his knowledge of Judaism was slight.[11] For Barrett, "If John by his words in this verse [11.49] (repeated emphatically in v.51 and 18.13) means that a high priest was appointed every year we must conclude that he was not a Jew."[12] Quite so. And Barrett's attempt to wriggle out of the conclusion is not plausible: "His words however do not necessarily bear this meaning. Probably he meant only that Caiaphas was high priest in that memorable year of our Lord's passion."[13] This meaning cannot readily be extracted from the Greek that is repeated twice more.[14]

11

THE

PARALYTIC

AT THE POOL

✠ ✠ ✠

I FIRST INTENDED NOT TO DEAL with the miracles performed on the Sabbath. Such appear in the Synoptics and John, and since they necessarily involve some hostility toward the Pharisaic tradition I felt it would not be easy to demonstrate the distinctive note of S in John (if it was there). In this I was mistaken. In the account of the healing of the paralytic in John 5, the hostility of Jesus toward Pharisaic Judaism is portrayed as going beyond anything in the Synoptics.

The lame and paralyzed man had no one to put him into the pool at Bethesda to be cured. Jesus asked if he wanted to be cured (5.6), and then said, "Rise, take your mat and walk" (5.8). This occurred on a Sabbath (5.9). Rabbinic tradition was firm. To heal by working on the Sabbath was unlawful unless the sickness was life threatening.[1] The paralytic had been sick for thirty-eight years, as we are expressly informed, so his illness could scarcely be regarded as immediately life threatening. Still, healing on the Sabbath was by itself not illegal.[2] But carrying was contrary to the prohibition against working on the Sabbath.[3] Accordingly, the former invalid was told by the Jews that his behavior was unlawful, and he responded that the one who had cured him had told him to take up his mat and walk (5.10f.).[4] Thus, Jesus was at fault, not for working on the Sabbath in curing the man, but for telling the sick man to carry his mat on the Sabbath. It should be noted that, for the paralytic, to obey the command to break the law was a prerequisite to the cure. Obviously, too, for a miracle worker to command the person to be healed to break the law is entirely unnecessary. Still, to this point, the account does not go too much beyond Sabbath cures in the Synoptics.

A detail of emphasis should, however, be noted. The express stress of the Pharisees' complaint about the breach of the Sabbath is the carrying of the mat: "You are not allowed to carry your bed on the Sabbath" (5.10); and "Who is the man who told you to take up your bed and walk?" (5.12). There is no expression of a breach of the Sabbath by healing the sick, and in this it is in contrast with the equivalent episodes in the Synoptics. Thus in Matthew 12.9ff., Jesus cures the withered hand on the Sabbath. There is no indication that this involved any of the forms of work set out in Mishnah Shabbath 7.2. Still, as a result and for the first time, the Pharisees conspire to kill him. The same is found in Mark 3.1ff., though this time the Herodians also seek to destroy him. Likewise in Luke 6.6ff., the Pharisees seek to accuse him following the cure. Again, on a Sabbath Jesus cured a woman crippled with a spirit for eighteen years, and no work seems to have been involved (Luke 13.11ff.).

But John now has Jesus going far beyond the limits of all propriety. The Jews persecute him for healing by forcing another to work on the Sabbath (5.16). He responds, "My Father is still working up to the present (ἕως ἄρτι), and I also am working" (5.17). This causes the Jews to seek all the more (μᾶλλον) to kill him (5.18).

The offense with which Jesus is charged is working (or causing others to work) on the Sabbath. His defense is that God is working and that what he himself does is no different. That is, his defense is that God also works on the Sabbath. But to claim that God works on the Sabbath is to deny the Sabbath, and without the Sabbath there can be no Judaism. The centrality of the Sabbath to

Judaism is shown in all the Gospels, even in the hostility to Jesus working on that day.

In Jewish tradition, God at times is said to continue working on the Sabbath.[5] Thus, Philo, a contemporary of Jesus, writes, "For God never leaves off making, but even as it is the property of fire to burn and of snow to chill, so it is the property of God to make: nay more so by far, inasmuch as he is to all besides the source of action."[6] But this continuing work of God on the Sabbath is never represented as ordinary, but spiritual, work. Philo also writes immediately before the passage just quoted: "First of all, then, on the seventh day the Creator, having brought to an end the formation of mortal things, begins the shaping of others more divine." God's work on the Sabbath is not man's work. Any belief that God worked on the Sabbath in this way would not mitigate Jesus' supposed offense. The accusation is that Jesus breached the Sabbath by working. And, as I mentioned earlier in this chapter, so according to rabbinic tradition he did. His defense is that God likewise works as he does on the Sabbath. Nor is Jesus' own belief in what he was doing a relevant factor. What matters is that for the Jews Jesus was breaking the Sabbath prohibition against working and he claimed that God does the same.

Thus, I would attribute this episode to S as well: Jesus is represented as speaking in a way that is (properly) intolerable to the Jews. John then has defanged S by adding his own message, changing the emphasis: "For this reason the Jews were seeking all the more (μαλλον) to kill him, because he was not only breaking the Sabbath, but was also calling God his own Father, thereby making himself equal to God" (5.18). So successful was John's defanging that modern commentators fail to notice that Jesus' defense was an attack on the whole notion of the Sabbath.[7] "All the more" to kill him in 5.18 is stressed because Jesus' offense in denying the Sabbath is much greater than that of causing the paralytic to work on the Sabbath, for which "the Jews started persecuting Jesus" (5.16).[8]

12

"HE WHO SAW THIS"

✠ ✠ ✠

EYEWITNESS TESTIMONY APPEARS only four times in the Gospels, three of these in John.

In his prologue Luke records:

> 1. Since many have undertaken to set down an orderly account of the events that have been fulfilled among us, 2. just as they were handed on to us by those who from the beginning were eyewitnesses and servants of the word, 3. I too decided, after investigating everything carefully from the very first, to write an orderly account for you, most excellent Theophilus, 4. so that you may know the truth concerning the things about which you have been instructed.

Eyewitnesses are not mentioned in Luke again. For present purposes, the important point is that these witnesses (who do not include the author of Luke) are not shown as eyewitnesses to a particular event. The same is true of two of the instances in John. Thus: "And the Word became flesh and lived among us, and we have seen his glory, the glory as of a father's only son, full of grace and truth" (1.14). This, indeed, is so vague that one must doubt whether John is talking about eyewitnesses to Jesus' life or generic witnesses to his glory. Chapter 21.24, though to a different effect, is no more precise: "This is the disciple who is testifying to these things and has written them, and we know that his testimony is true." This disciple is identified in 21.20: he was known to Peter and was, indeed, "the disciple whom Jesus loved." His testimony is to his whole Gospel.

The remaining instance is very different, and it has already surfaced in chapter 9.

19.31. Since it was the day of Preparation, the Jews did not want the bodies left on the cross during the sabbath, especially because that sabbath was a day of great solemnity. So they asked Pilate to have the legs of the crucified men broken and the bodies removed. 32. Then the soldiers came and broke the legs of the first and of the other who had been crucified with him. 33. But when they came to Jesus and saw that he was already dead, they did not break his legs. 34. Instead, one of the soldiers pierced his side with a spear, and at once blood and water came out. 35. (He who saw this has testified so that you also may believe. His testimony is true, and he knows that he tells the truth). 36. These things occurred so that the scripture might be fulfilled, "None of his bones shall be broken." 37. And again another passage of scripture says, "They will look on the one whom they have pierced."

As the sole precise episode where eyewitness testimony is stressed, the testimony must have particular significance.[1] If the stress is somehow connected with S, then we are faced with two possibilities. Either the stress was in S because the testimony was particularly damaging to Christianity, in which case the testimony was that Jesus' legs were broken. Or the redactor of John changed the substance of S in which Jesus' legs were shown to be broken and added the emphasis that they were not broken. I have already preferred the latter. If Jesus' legs were broken, then his resurrection would be hindered and John would have good reason for insisting that they were not: this view is supported by 19.36. Still, the choice does not much matter.

But now we must go further. The much controverted[2] apocryphal Gospel of Peter describes the Crucifixion:

> 4.13. *But one of the malefactors* rebuked them, saying, *"We have landed in suffering for the deeds of wickedness which we have committed, but this man*, who has become the savior of men, what wrong has he done you?" And they were wroth with him and commanded that his *legs* should not be broken, so that he might die in torments.[3]

This is very different from the account in John, and it is the main reason that persuaded P. Gardner-Smith that the author of Peter did not know the Gospel of John.[4] On the other hand, the most influential current theory is perhaps that of J. D. Crossan, who believes that at the earliest stage, the Gospel of Peter—called for this stage by Crossan the *Cross Gospel*—was used by all four canonical Gospels.[5]

For present purposes we need not decide whether the author of Peter knew John, or whether John used an early version of Peter, or whether John or Peter was earlier. What matters is the tradition in Peter.

The breaking of a malefactor's legs on the cross is well attested. Its purpose was to mitigate the penalty by hastening the painful lingering death. In Peter, the executioners, angered by one brigand, decided not to break his legs in order to increase and prolong his torment. The clear implication is that the other two on the cross, including Jesus, did have their legs broken. Thus, there did exist a tradition that of the three who were crucified, two had their legs broken; one of these men was Jesus. It was such a tradition found also in S, where it was used as an argument against Jesus' resurrection, that John was combating in claiming to have eyewitness testimony. The need for John's emphatic claim is confirmed.

Since S has not hitherto been recognized as a source of John, standard interpretations cannot take it into account, and a completely different explanation of the incident has to be given, an explanation that owes nothing to the belief current in Jesus' time that mutilation of the body hindered resurrection. Such interpretations account for John's emphasis on eyewitnessing by pointing to a theological message. For the most part, these theological interpretations link Jesus with the paschal lamb, as the Lamb of God.[6] The Septuagint (*codex Vaticanus*) of Exodus 12.10, but not the Hebrew Bible, has in the description of the paschal lamb, "You shall not break a bone of it." Exodus 12.46 has, "You shall not break any of its bones"; though the animal is not specified, it is a lamb. This is reiterated in Numbers 9.12. A further cause of identification of Jesus with the paschal lamb is that in Exodus 12.8 and Numbers 9.11, the lamb is to be eaten with "bitter herbs," and Jesus on the cross was given to drink sour wine "on a branch of hyssop." There is not much in all of this to make clear the image of Jesus as the Passover lamb.[7] Moreover, the notion of the Messiah, the Redeemer, or the Son of God as the Passover lamb or the Lamb of God nowhere appears in the Old Testament or in the Synoptic Gospels. Indeed, even in John the concept is expressed only in the introduction— John the Baptist declares of Jesus, "Behold, the Lamb of God, who takes away the sin of the world" (1.29); "Behold, the Lamb of God" (1.36). The great success of the symbolism of the suffering Jesus as the Lamb of God is later and is entirely due to John.[8] I am not suggesting that this symbolism is absent from John, but only that it is oblique and by itself would not explain John's extreme insistence that Jesus' legs were not broken.

Nor surprisingly, many distinguished scholars see a different symbolism in the incident,[9] that in Psalm 34.20: "He keeps all his bones [i.e., of the righteous afflicted]; not one of them is broken." For me it is even more difficult to explain the unique emphasis in John as the result of this verse.

John's emphasis is also on the piercing of Jesus' side with a lance: "And again another passage of scripture says, 'They will look upon the one they have pierced'" (19.37). This seems a reference to the obscure verse, Zechariah 12.10: "And I will pour out a spirit of compassion and supplication on the house of David and the inhabitants of Jerusalem, so that, when they look on the one whom they have pierced, they shall mourn for him, as one mourns for an only child, and weep bitterly over him, as one weeps over a firstborn." There is not enough in this, I think, to explain or justify the unique emphasis on eyewitness testimony that is found in John 19. Indeed, the text is not an ideal fit. In Zechariah, it is the house of David and Jerusalem who have done the piercing; in John 19.34, it is a Roman soldier.[10]

My argument is that the unique emphasis in John on Jesus' legs not being broken demands explanation. My conclusion is that the emphasis was needed to counteract an anti-Christian tradition that Jesus' legs were, indeed, broken and that this was regarded as an obstacle to resurrection. Such a conclusion would provide some confirmation that in Johannine tradition there was a source such as S and that, in fact, it was used here. We do know from the Gospel of Peter that even in some Christian traditions Jesus' legs were broken. But the differences between Peter and what I claim for S must be set out. In Peter we are left to infer that Jesus' legs were broken: the fact is incidental and would not provoke an emphatic, unique eyewitness denial. In S, that Jesus' legs were broken is a central fact and would provoke the eyewitness denial.

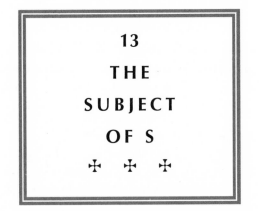

13

THE

SUBJECT

OF S

✠ ✠ ✠

AT ONE STAGE I thought it likely that S was used in other episodes, but the work of the redactor could have skillfully concealed its presence. I avoided dealing with some instances where I felt the arguments were less clear-cut than in the episodes in the preceding chapters. Even in the episodes discussed, I have avoided pushing my arguments to the limit. I have also avoided sideshows, so as not to divert attention from the main point.

But now I want to go back to the meeting of Jesus and the Samaritan woman, to argue that S's presence was greater than I previously suggested. After Jesus remarks that the man with whom the Samaritan is living is not her husband, the text continues (4.19ff.):

> The woman said to him, "Sir, I see that you are a prophet.
> 20. Our ancestors worshiped on this mountain, but you say that the place where people must worship is in Jerusalem."
> 21. Jesus said to her, "Woman, believe me, the hour is coming when you will worship the Father neither on this mountain nor in Jerusalem. 22. You worship what you do not know; we worship what we know, for salvation is from the Jews. 23. But the hour is coming, and is now here, when the true worshipers will worship the Father in spirit and truth, for the Father seeks such as these to worship him. 24. God is spirit, and those who

worship him must worship in spirit and truth." 25. The woman said to him, "I know that Messiah is coming" (he who is called Christ). "When he comes, he will proclaim all things to us." 26. Jesus said to her, "I am he, the one who is speaking to you."

"Salvation is from the Jews." This is certainly not the message of John. For Rudolf Bultmann this is a gloss.[1] The problem for me is to understand when, by whom, in what circumstances, such a gloss contrary to the whole message could have been added. For me, the words indicate the use of S, and their import was overlooked. This is a much simpler explanation. Raymond Brown has a more complex explanation, and he does, in fact, put considerable emphasis on the text.[2] For him, this is Jesus talking to a foreigner about the whole Jewish people, not about the leaders. It is, Brown claims, a clear indication that the Johannine attitude was not modern anti-Semitism or a rejection of the spiritual heritage of Judaism. That it derives from S is, in my view, still a much simpler explanation because the verse goes beyond Brown's claim. Jesus tells the Samaritan that he is the Messiah (4.26). This is the only occasion in John when Jesus tells anyone that he is the Messiah, and he tells not a Jew but one of the hated Samaritans.[3] The text must be contrasted with 10.23ff.: "and Jesus was walking in the temple, in the portico of Solomon. 24. So the Jews gathered around him and said to him, 'How long will you keep us in suspense? If you are the Messiah, tell us plainly.' 25. Jesus answered, 'I have told you, and you do not believe, because you do not belong to my sheep.'" He will not give a straight answer to the Jews (though he comes close with Martha in 11.25f.).

The woman left Jesus and went back to her city. "Come and see a man who told me everything I have ever done! He cannot be the Messiah, can he?" (4.29). In keeping with her disgraced status in her community, the woman seeks to regain favor and ingratiate herself. She fails, but the people go to see Jesus and are convinced, anyway. "They said to the woman, 'It is no longer because of what you said that we believe, for we have heard for ourselves, and we know that this is truly the Savior of the world'" (4.42).

It seems to me that in all this, too, we might detect the influence of S. Jesus is willing to claim to one of the hated Samaritans that he is the Messiah. But he makes no such claim to the Jews: either he does not dare to, or he does not wish to enlighten them. Samaritans, benighted as they are, believe him. Yet elsewhere we are told that because of his extreme claims many of his Jewish followers left him (6.66). Indeed, it is stressed that not even his brothers believed in him (7.5). The hated Samaritans do believe, but wretched and mean-spirited as they are, this does not persuade them to forgive the woman who led them to Jesus. Thus, the very Jewish S, which is always hostile to Jesus who is ever portrayed as the enemy of the Jews, makes him say that salvation will come from the Jews. He convinces the Samaritans that he is the Messiah, but that does not make them better people.

In John, in the context of S, Jesus takes his message to the Samaritans. In contrast, in Matthew 10.5f.—and there is no S in Matthew—we find: "These twelve Jesus sent out, charging them, 'Go nowhere among the Gentiles, and enter no town of the Samaritans, 6. but go rather to the lost sheep of the house of Israel.'"[4]

A text important in this connection is John 8.48. "The Jews answered him, 'Are we not right in saying that you are a Samaritan and have a demon?'" I have no wish to attribute this text. In isolating Jesus from the Jews and associating him with the Samaritans, it is in line with S. But the slur is put in the mouth of the Jews and may be part of John's anti-Jewishness.

In chapter 16 I will set out in different typefaces the main passages I have discussed, to show clearly what I believe are their origins, in S, in the redactor, or in some unattributed source. When preparing that chapter I did, in fact, make such a scheme for the whole of John. When I extracted both S and the redactor with his theological message, what was left surprised me. Apart from the washing of the disciples' feet (13.3ff.), there was really nothing which did not have its counterpart in the Synoptics. The remaining episodes of activity had nothing striking in them. Indeed, they appear rather flat. The episodes with parallels in the Synoptics are curing the official's son (4.46ff.), feeding the multitude with loaves and fishes (6.1ff.)[5] Jesus walking on the water (6.16ff.), enabling the blind man to see on the Sabbath (9.1ff.), the woman anointing Jesus with costly perfumes (12.3ff.), the arrest, Crucifixion (in general), and Resurrection.[6]

At this point I should like to return with a conjecture to the end of chapter 1, to the relationship of John to the Synoptics. I still accept the validity of Robert Grant's argument that no proof is possible establishing the nature of this relationship. Still, I should like to suggest that John was very aware of the Synoptics. A strange feature of John's treatment of the episodes in Jesus' life is precisely the dominance that has emerged of the hostile source that I have called S. Why? I would suggest that, whether or not there were two stages of theological message in John (and in 1 John and 2 John), the redactor wrote with two main purposes. First, he set forth his theological message. Second, he defanged and incorporated S (I'll take this matter further in chapter 15). He had no need to devote much space or attention to other episodic sources precisely because they could be taken for granted: they were well known to his audience and, accordingly, to himself. The plausibility, or otherwise, of this conjecture should not affect the general arguments in this book.

But if in these episodes in John I could find no real trace of S, whereas I believe I did in other episodes, might it be possible to contrast the two sets in order to isolate the main subject matter of S? I have already categorized that source, but might it not also have subject matter that could be uncovered? The subject matter of S, I suggest, is the story of a man, Jesus, at odds with the law, continually breaking the law, who nonetheless was met by restraint on the part of the authorities until he put the survival of the whole Jewish people in jeopardy. He prevented the water jars at Cana from being used for ritual purification, he violently drove religious helpers out of the Temple precincts, he drank from a ritually unclean vessel, and he entered into conversation with an unclean woman. He broke the Sabbath by working, coerced another into breaking the Sabbath, and denied the Sabbath. He posed as the Messiah or the Son of God. Nonetheless, the Jewish authorities took no determined action—although they were perturbed—until it appeared that his continued behavior would destroy the nation. Even then, they arranged to have the Romans execute him for a crime against the Romans. The instigators of this were the Sadducees, not the Pharisees, yet Jesus is shown as opposed not to the Sadducees but to the Pharisees, who took the view that the written law was developed by the oral law that was also binding.

Thus, the main but not exclusive subject of S is law in action. S is the product of lawyers: scribes and Pharisees.[7]

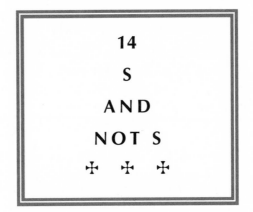

14

S

AND

NOT S

✠ ✠ ✠

THOUGH IN THE EPISODES from Jesus' life S is prominent and even dominant, it does not stand alone as a source. Here, to point a contrast, I want to examine one episode, giving sight to the man blind from birth (9.1ff.), which in my view is free from traces of S.

While my main interest is in the differences between S and other episodic sources, I must also stress similarities. Without these, S could not have been successfully used by John. Where differences remain, thus revealing the existence of S, John has failed.

On a Sabbath Jesus and his disciples met a man blind from birth (9.1). Jesus, apparently taking the initiative, spat on the ground and made a paste from the mud. He thus broke the Sabbath prohibition against working: specifically, kneading is one of the thirty-nine forms of work in Mishnah Shabbath 7.2. Though Jesus then told the man to wash in the pool of Siloam (9.7), nothing indicates that he urged the man to break the law. Nor in what follows is there any indication that the Pharisees blamed the man for participating in his cure. He was brought before the Pharisees, and he explained what had happened (9.13ff.). The Pharisees were divided in their opinion. For some, Jesus was not from God because he broke the Sabbath. For others, a sinner could not perform such miracles (9.16). In the end they decided not to accept that this was the man born blind, and they made further inquiries (9.18ff.).

In what follows, the source stresses the fear that ordinary Jews had of the Pharisees' anger. The blind man's parents admit he is their son and was born blind, but declare that they do not know how he was cured (9.20ff.). This is reasonable enough, except that they insist the Pharisees should ask their son himself because he is of age. The Pharisees are scary thought police.[1]

The Pharisees resume questioning the man who had been blind (9.24ff.). He refuses to concede that Jesus was a sinner and insists that what he did know was that he had been blind but now he could see (9.25). To further interrogation he insists that he had told them all before: "Why do you want to hear it again? Do you also want to become his disciples?" (9.27). There is humor in this, perhaps of a desperate kind, as also in his statement, "Here is an astonishing thing! You do not know where he comes from, and yet he opened my eyes" (9.30). He also claims that God does not listen to sinners (9.31), and maintains, "If this man were not from God, he could do nothing" (9.33). The Pharisees' response is to declare that the blind man was born in utter sin, and they cast him out (9.34).

At this stage we may pause to consider how the telling of this episode corresponds to those from S. In both, Jesus breaks the law by working in a good cause on the Sabbath. But this time he does nothing more and says nothing that is offensive. He does not cause the blind man to break the law; he does not blaspheme or deny the Sabbath. Far from that, he denies that the blindness was caused by sin (9.3), although at that time it was still held by some that sickness was the result of sinning whether by the individual or by his parents.[2] On the other hand, it is the Pharisees who adopt that harsh view and claim the man was born steeped in sin, and they eject him. We are probably not justified in treating this as expulsion from the synagogue, but only from their presence.[3] Still, expulsion from the synagogue had already been threatened for any who confessed Jesus to be the Messiah (9.22).[4] There are no mitigating factors in their behavior. Even worse, the Pharisees are in part motivated by anger that a sinner was daring to teach them (9.34). Again, humor, even of a bitter kind, is entirely lacking in the texts I have identified as being from S. It occurs again, though, in 6.26: "Very truly, I tell you, you are looking for me, not because you saw signs but because you ate your fill of the loaves."

Later, Jesus converses with the former blind man (9.35ff.) and is overheard by some Pharisees, who ask, "Surely we are not blind, are we?" Jesus replies, "If you were blind, you would not have sin. But now that you say, 'We see,' your sin remains" (9.41). Throughout the episode, the same motif recurs: blindness, sight, sin. For Jesus, the afflicted man's blindness was not caused by sin, and he heals him. Jesus declares, "I am the light of the world" (9.5). The Pharisees claim that the blindness proved the man was born steeped in sin. Jesus tells the Pharisees that if they were blind they would not have sin, but because they insist that they see, their sin remains. The details of the story and the theological message are interwoven in a way, and to an extent, that I find missing in S. More than that, no detail here seems out of place in John's overall message.

One problem that often surfaces when one is considering rabbinic law in the New Testament is that the surviving rabbinic sources are later and may not represent the law in the time of Jesus. That issue should be made express, though it has scarcely arisen in this book for the obvious reason that on the basic matters we have evidence for the existence of the relevant law. Thus, for the wedding feast at Cana we know there was an obligation to wash one's hands before eating (Matthew 15.1–3; Mark 7.1–4; Luke 11.37f.). That Jews did not use vessels used by Samaritans appears from the episode itself at 4.9. That, by touching Jesus' corpse, Nicodemus would become ritually unclean and unable to eat the Passover meal is attested by Numbers 19.11f. and in the episode itself at 18.28. The prohibitions against working on the Sabbath are emphasized in numerous texts, and the interpretation of these appears in the very contexts of the stories.

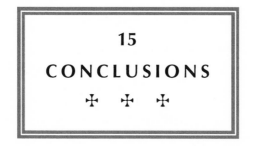

15
CONCLUSIONS
✠ ✠ ✠

THIS WORK DID NOT START OFF as a book. Rather, my attention was caught by details in the encounter of Jesus with the Samaritan woman that suggested a subtext. Details seemed to lurk that did not portray Jesus in the best of lights and that were inconsistent with the theological message of John. I examined that episode by itself and published some conclusions. Eventually, I decided to look at the other episodes that occurred only in John, examining each separately, and drawing no argument from one to another. The interpretation of each should be able to stand on its own. In each I saw details that did not fit the general picture of John.

When I put the odd or inconsistent details together, I believed I had found among the sources of John one powerful strand (S) that portrayed Jesus as a miracle worker but also as a flawed human being who was virulently and needlessly hostile to Jewish law and tradition and even a great danger to Jewish existence. This source, it seemed to me, was Jewish and inimical to Christianity. The leaders of the Jews were even shown as objectively justified in seeking Jesus' death.

But the finding had to be checked against other material. It is too easy in form criticism to be selective, ignoring opposing data and exaggerating the inconsistencies one thinks one has uncovered. So a first check was run against the other three Gospels. I found nothing in Matthew, Mark, or Luke that seemed to correspond to my S for John. Certainly, Jesus was portrayed as opposed to Jewish emphasis on ritual and formalism, but not to anything like the degree he showed in the four Johannine episodes. Nor did he have anything like the flaws he had in S. It thus seemed more certain that there was a particular source used in John but not in the Synoptics. I then ran a second check. In those episodes that occurred in John and in at least one Synoptic, but where John's version was significantly different, were there details in John indicative of the use of a source like that I had thought I had uncovered in the four episodes? Such details did seem to exist. S was apparent in John elsewhere than in the four episodes, further confirmation that there was such a source. When the episodes in which S appeared in John were contrasted with those in which there was no trace of S, it emerged that a major subject of S was Jesus as a man at odds with the law. And religious law is law as truth.

The argument for the existence of a source such as S is entirely plausible. When a supposed Messiah or God arises in a society, and some believe and others do not, there will be a conflict of views. Episodes and arguments that Jesus was God would be met with others showing that he was not. The same episodes could be used, with differing emphasis, to prove each side's case. But, as in a lawsuit, so in such a hothouse of religious debate, one side could not ignore the evidence produced by the other. The contrary evidence had to be considered, to show that the wrong conclusions had been drawn from it. In the environment in which the redactor was working, John could not ignore S, just as S could not deny to Jesus the status of miracle worker. But John could take S, change the emphasis, and present a different message. But just as S could not go too far in obvious hostility to Jesus without being entirely discounted by the uncommitted, so John had to keep to the tradition of S to counteract it. Inevitably, as with other composite works, the tendency of S as a separate source can still be uncovered.

In chapter 7 I quoted Raymond Brown on the peril of positing supposed—he has "nonexistent"—pre-Gospel sources and then placing within the source harmonious theological material. I wish here to insist that my approach has been very different. For example, my argument that the woman of Samaria was trying to seduce Jesus is, in my original paper, independent of any hypothesis of S. Again, the idea that peculiar tensions overshadow the miracle at Cana has long been recognized. The problem is to account for them, not to find them. That Jesus' raising Lazarus from the dead poses a threat to the Temple and the Jewish nation and that this fully explains, and even justifies, the Jews' desire to have Jesus executed requires no hypothesis of S. Likewise, Jesus' denial of the Sabbath when the paralytic is enabled to walk goes beyond the limit of tolerable behavior on any explanation. My claim is that S—in all its complexities, including the noble Nicodemus as counterpoint to the gross Jesus—takes shape and emerges as a pre-Gospel source because of oddities in the text that are otherwise recognizable.

Skeptics may object, as they have for Q, "Where is the literary evidence?"[1] Of course, I cannot produce independently surviving fragments of texts. But the hypothesis rests on its overall plausibility. John must have used earlier sources. Some episodes as we have them contain unlikely and disharmonious elements, out of keeping with John's theological message. But they present a consistent picture. The principle of Occam's razor suggests they belong together in a source such as S.

I have tried to avoid further deduction from the hypothesis of S. Still, if the hypothesis is correct, light will be shed on John's historical setting and theological message. Along the way three points did, in fact, emerge. First, S was a source in Greek, not in Aramaic. The presence of Semitisms in John is in no way decisive for Aramaic because such could be used in the Greek of a particular society as a result of linguistic tradition. What does matter is that in Nicodemus's first encounter with Jesus, there was a vital misunderstanding that could occur in Greek but not in a Semitic language. That the evangelist wrote in Greek also entails that he was working in a Greek-speaking environment. There was no point in him writing in Greek if the people around him knew no Greek. Second, it appeared that John did not know Judaism "from the inside." In a composite work in which the individual sources are not identified, statements of fact that are correct do not show the final redactor's state of personal knowledge. They could derive from the sources. But in contrast, statements of fact that are wrong do betray the redactor's ignorance. He had the last chance to correct the mistake. Thus, if there are in John twenty details that are accurate about Judaism, and one that is a howler, repeated three times, and one that is a gaffe, then what is accurate must not be attributed to the personal knowledge of the redactor. Third, John was written for a circle not all of whose members were fast in their Christianity. Others may have been simply seekers after truth, some perhaps even hostile. There were also Jews in the area. The argument for this is simply that John used S. To use and manipulate a hostile witness, a technique that can always go wrong, makes sense only when the witness cannot be ignored.

It is fitting that I outline my idea of the background against which John was written. But I must stress that I have not used this concept of the historical background in reconstructing S. Indeed, only when I had completed the rest of the book did I turn to the issue of John's audience. It will be observed that my history is in several ways close to that of Raymond Brown.[2]

In or near Palestine, Jews, including followers of John the Baptist, who were waiting for the Messiah, accepted Jesus as such and found this confirmed by his miracles. They were joined by others, including converts from Samaria, and there was debate among themselves as to the precise nature of Jesus. There was also much debate with Jews who did not accept that Jesus was the Messiah or the Son of God. Each side to the debate, those who believed in Christ and those who did not, developed traditions and sources, at least to some extent in writing, setting out their position. S, in its primitive version, was a product of those Jews who were hostile to

Christianity and, in particular, of Pharisees. Eventually, the leaders of the Jews had the Christians expelled from the Synagogue. The above events occurred between the fifties and the late eighties.

These Christians, expelled from the Synagogue, reacted hostilely to those Jews within and emphasized the ministry to the world at large. They probably lived in a Greek-speaking part of the diaspora. It was then around A.D. 90 that John was written in Greek. The redactor and his community were close enough to the preceding conflict with "the Jews" that they had to come face to face with the tradition of S and confront it. The version of S, probably written, that was used was also in Greek. This is an indication that wherever the Gospel was written, there was a sizable population of Jews who held to their faith. But the redactor at least was sufficiently removed from Palestinian Jewry to make grave mistakes about their organization.

It may be noted in passing that references to "the Jews" must come from a time after the expulsion of the Christians from the synagogue. Only then would Christians not regard themselves as also Jews.[3]

From time to time it is still argued that the evangelist John is John, the son of Zebedee, or some other disciple, and that the Gospel of John is not a composite work.[4] I do not find that view plausible. One would have to argue that the references to "the Jews" are later insertions, and John's mistakes over Palestinian Judaism would be inexplicable. There is the problem that the Gospel seems to have been written in Greek.[5] But from my perspective what is interesting is how little my basic arguments would be affected. The thesis would be different—S would be John—but the arguments would be the same. It would be John the disciple who experienced Jesus the charismatic miracle worker—and Son of God—who, however, also behaved at times violently and unsympathetically and who was, indeed, a deliberate violator in the most hostile way of Jewish tradition. It would be the same writer who, in contempt for Jewish ritual, did not mention the guests' angry reaction to Jesus' misuse of the water in the purification jars at Cana. John would have accurately portrayed Jesus' violence in cleansing the Temple, and Matthew, Mark, and Luke would have toned this down. John would have correctly represented the Last Supper, and Matthew, Mark, and Luke would have turned it into a Passover dinner, adding the Eucharist detail to show that Jesus was the Messiah. Jesus would then be very much the son of his father. Jehovah himself, it will be remembered, was known to be occasionally violent and unsympathetic: like father, like son. Jesus would be a loyal son, who was upset that his father's law was misinterpreted. Jehovah lacks civility. So in S does Jesus. If S is the disciple John, then what demands an explanation is the civility of Jesus in those episodes in John that I do not attribute to S. As I said, I find implausible the view that the evangelist John was John the son of Zebedee. But if I had accepted it, I could have written a very similar book. And it would have been much more entertaining.

An argument favoring the view that Jesus' incivility in John was his true nature as seen by his followers and does not derive from a hostile Jewish source is that to some degree Jesus lacks civility at times also in other Gospels. The best example, I think, is in Matthew 15:

21. Jesus left that place and went away to the district of Tyre and Sidon. 22. Just then a Canaanite woman from that region came out and started shouting, "Have mercy on me, Lord, Son of David; my daughter is tormented by a demon." 23. But he did not answer her at all. And his disciples came and urged him, saying, "Send her away, for she keeps shouting after us." 24. He answered, "I was sent only to the lost sheep of the house of Israel." 25. But she came and knelt before him, saying, "Lord, help me." 26. He answered, "It is not fair to take the children's food and throw it to the dogs." 27. She said, "Yes, Lord, yet even the dogs eat the crumbs that fall from their masters' table." 28. Then Jesus answered her, "Woman,

great is your faith! Let it be done for you as you wish." And her daughter was healed instantly.

Here the "children" are the Jews, and the "dogs" are all others. Jesus and his disciples at first do not respond to the anguished pleas of a Canaanite woman. Then he responds rudely: "It is not fair to take the children's food and throw it to the dogs." The message that his healing was only for the Jews, harsh though that may be, could have been phrased courteously. It is only the woman's clever response that wins him over to help her. Despite all that, it remains the case that Jesus' incivility is much more marked in John. And in Matthew 15, he does change his mind and cure the woman's daughter.

If we accept the existence of a source such as S and that the evangelist had to deal with it, then the arrangement of John itself is part of a literary masterpiece. Jesus is introduced to the audience as the Lamb of God by John the Baptist, who has already been questioned by the Pharisees, and the two disciples with John follow Jesus (1.29–37). The stage is set. Jesus collects more disciples (1.43ff.) and performs his first miracle at the wedding feast at Cana (2.1ff.). In S this miracle was to show how flawed Jesus was; now it reveals his glory to the disciples. Its minor nature is a counterpoint to the final and greatest miracle, the raising of Lazarus. Jesus cleanses the Temple (2.13ff.). In S this typified Jesus' hostility to Jewish ritual and law; now it is a protest against the trivialization of religion. Jesus performs unspecified signs (2.23). Nicodemus comes to Jesus at night (3.1ff.). In S this is to show the perfect Pharisee in contrast to the imperfect Jesus; in John the encounter leads to Jesus' first ecstatic discourse. Birth into the kingdom of God through water (baptism: 3.5) and spirit leads into the Baptist's discussion with a Jew about baptism and the Spirit (3.25ff.). The meeting with the Samaritan woman at the well in S showed a Jesus hostile to Jewish ritual cleanliness who led a sinful woman on; in John, Jesus takes his message to the non-Jew, the

weak and the sinner.[6] Jesus performs another miracle, again curing
the child of a non-Jew (4.46ff.). Jesus heals a paralytic, breaching
the Sabbath; in S he is denying Judaism; in John he is putting the
Jews in a bad light because they want to kill him (5.1ff.). After a
discourse on Jesus' relation to God (5.19ff.), we have more miracles
told rather flatly (6.1ff.)—in my opinion this is *because* they were
in the Synoptics—and Jesus teaches in the Temple (7.14ff.). The
Pharisees seek to have him arrested (7.32ff.). Again we have a
spiritual discourse (8.12ff.)—Jesus the light of the world—and a
blind man is made to see on the Sabbath (9.1ff.). The Pharisees are
shown as nasty and blind. Jesus declares he is the good shepherd
(10.1–18). The Jews again seek to stone him (10.31ff.). He performs
his greatest miracle, raising Lazarus from the dead. This leads on
to the beautiful progression of events already set out at the end of
chapter 9. When a time is mentioned within an episode in John it
is significant, but the redactor has no interest in the absolute chronology of episodes: they are moved around to meet aesthetic and
theological needs.

At this late stage in the book I want to take my argument further. To this point I have been content to argue that John made use
of S because he had no choice: S was a hostile witness who had to
be dealt with. But S has also emerged as John's main narrative
source. I want now to claim that John did not want simply to
defang S, the hostile witness. On the contrary, he deliberately
made use of the hostile witness to proclaim triumphantly his message about Jesus: from the testimony of the enemy arises the larger
theological truth.[7]

16

S

✛ ✛ ✛

IT IS NOT MY PURPOSE in this penultimate chapter to produce new arguments or evidence. My goal is simply to set out for clarity's sake the major texts I have discussed to show how far S can be isolated and how few changes John (or a predecessor) needed to make in order to destroy its thrust and insert his own. I am not claiming that the redactor of John had a manuscript of S in front of him and copied it *verbatim* except when he was deliberately making changes. We have no independent evidence of his use of such sources. But his account of episodes in the life of Jesus had to be plausible in the context of traditions about Jesus in the place where the redactor was working.[1] Moreover, scholars have long known that John is much more specific that the Synoptics when it refers to places. When John can be checked against archaeological evidence, it proves to be remarkably accurate: thus, the pool at the sheep gate (5.2) does, in fact, have five porticoes. Gabbatha, where Pilate sat on the tribunal (19.13), can be recognized, which indicates that John (indeed, S) has local knowledge that goes back beyond the destruction of the Temple in A.D. 70.[2] Such accuracy is inconsistent with cavalier treatment of a source such as S.

One point that I want to stress is how simple the task was to defang S and incorporate it into John, compared with the task, as envisaged by modern Roman lawyers, that faced Justinian's compilers of the *Digest* in bringing the juristic texts of the Roman empire to A.D. 235 up to date for sixth-century Byzantium. Two examples, out of literally hundreds of thousands, of the complex relationships between original sources and the redactors of the *Digest* are set out in chapter 17. In comparison, incorporating S into John was, as we say in Glasgow, a dawdle.

With two small changes I will for simplicity use throughout in this chapter the translation of *The New English Bible*. The text of S is printed here in capital letters. Passages that I believe have been deleted from S are printed in capital letters within square parentheses. The text of the redactor, or a source so close to the redactor as to be indistinguishable, is set out in italics. Linking passages and passages not clearly attributable to the redactor are set out in plain face.

I.

2.1. ON THE THIRD DAY THERE WAS A WEDDING IN CANA-IN-GALILEE. 2. THE MOTHER OF JESUS WAS THERE, AND JESUS AND HIS DISCIPLES WERE GUESTS ALSO. 3. THE WINE GAVE OUT, SO JESUS'S MOTHER SAID TO HIM, "THEY HAVE NO WINE LEFT." 4. HE ANSWERED, "YOUR CONCERN, WOMAN,[3] IS NOT MINE. *My hour has not yet come."* 5. HIS MOTHER SAID TO THE SERVANTS, "DO WHATEVER HE TELLS YOU." 6. THERE WERE SIX STONE WATER-JARS STANDING NEAR, OF THE KIND USED FOR JEWISH RITES OF PURIFICATION; EACH HELD FROM TWENTY TO THIRTY GALLONS. 7. JESUS SAID TO THE SERVANTS, "FILL THE JARS WITH WATER," AND THEY FILLED THEM TO THE BRIM. 8. "NOW DRAW SOME OFF," HE ORDERED, "AND TAKE IT TO THE STEWARD OF THE FEAST"; AND THEY DID SO. 9. THE STEWARD TASTED THE WATER NOW TURNED INTO WINE, NOT KNOWING ITS SOURCE; THOUGH THE SERVANTS WHO HAD DRAWN THE WATER KNEW. 10. HE HAILED THE BRIDEGROOM AND SAID, "EVERYONE SERVES THE BEST WINE FIRST, AND WAITS UNTIL THE GUESTS HAVE DRUNK FREELY BEFORE SERVING THE POORER SORT; BUT YOU HAVE KEPT THE BEST WINE TILL NOW." [HOSTILE REACTION OF AFFRONTED GUESTS].

11. *This deed at Cana-in-Galilee is the first of the signs by which Jesus revealed his glory and led his disciples to believe in him.*

12. After this he went down to Capernaum in company with his mother, his brothers, and his disciples, but they did not stay there long.

II.

4.4. HE HAD TO PASS THROUGH SAMARIA, AND ON HIS WAY CAME TO A SAMARITAN TOWN CALLED SYCHAR, 5. NEAR THE PLOT OF GROUND WHICH JACOB GAVE TO HIS SON JOSEPH AND THE SPRING 6. CALLED JACOB'S WELL. IT WAS ABOUT NOON, AND JESUS, TIRED AFTER HIS JOURNEY, SAT DOWN BY THE WELL.

7. THE DISCIPLES HAD GONE AWAY TO THE TOWN TO BUY FOOD. 8. MEANWHILE A SAMARITAN WOMAN CAME TO DRAW WATER. JESUS SAID TO HER, "GIVE ME A DRINK." 9. THE SAMARITAN WOMAN SAID, "WHAT! YOU, A JEW, ASK A DRINK OF ME, A SAMARITAN WOMAN?" (Jews and Samaritans, it should be noted, do not use vessels in common.) 10. JESUS ANSWERED HER, "IF ONLY YOU KNEW *what God gives, and* WHO IT IS THAT IS ASKING YOU FOR A DRINK, YOU WOULD HAVE ASKED HIM AND HE WOULD HAVE GIVEN YOU LIVING WATER." 11. "SIR," THE WOMAN SAID, "YOU HAVE NO BUCKET AND THIS WELL IS DEEP. HOW CAN YOU GIVE ME 'LIVING WATER'? 12. ARE YOU A GREATER MAN THAN JACOB OUR ANCESTOR, WHO GAVE US THE WELL, AND DRANK FROM IT HIMSELF, HE AND HIS SONS, AND HIS CATTLE, TOO?" 13. JESUS SAID, "EVERYONE WHO DRINKS THIS WATER WILL BE THIRSTY AGAIN, 14. BUT WHOEVER DRINKS THE WATER THAT I SHALL GIVE WILL NEVER SUFFER THIRST ANY MORE. *The water that I shall give him will be an inner spring always welling up for eternal life."*

15. "SIR," SAID THE WOMAN, "GIVE ME THAT WATER, AND THEN I SHALL NOT BE THIRSTY, NOR HAVE TO COME ALL THIS WAY TO DRAW."

16. JESUS REPLIED, "GO HOME, CALL YOUR HUSBAND AND COME BACK." 17. SHE ANSWERED, "I HAVE NO HUSBAND." "YOU ARE RIGHT," SAID JESUS, "IN SAYING THAT YOU HAVE NO HUSBAND, FOR, AL-

THOUGH YOU HAVE HAD FIVE HUSBANDS, 18. THE MAN WITH WHOM
YOU ARE NOW LIVING IS NOT YOUR HUSBAND; YOU TOLD ME THE
TRUTH THERE." 19. "SIR," SHE REPLIED, "I CAN SEE THAT YOU ARE A
PROPHET. 20. OUR FATHERS WORSHIPPED ON THIS MOUNTAIN, BUT
YOU JEWS SAY THAT THE TEMPLE WHERE GOD SHOULD BE WORSHIPPED
IS IN JERUSALEM." 21. "BELIEVE ME," SAID JESUS, "THE TIME IS
COMING WHEN YOU WILL WORSHIP THE FATHER NEITHER ON THIS
MOUNTAIN, NOR IN JERUSALEM. 22. YOU SAMARITANS WORSHIP
WITHOUT KNOWING WHAT YOU WORSHIP, WHILE WE WORSHIP WHAT
WE KNOW. IT IS FROM THE JEWS THAT SALVATION COMES. 23. *But the
time approaches, indeed it is already here, when those who are
real worshippers will worship the Father in spirit and in truth.
Such are the worshippers whom the Father wants. 24. God is spirit,
and those who worship him must worship in spirit and in truth."*
25. THE WOMAN ANSWERED, "I KNOW THAT MESSIAH" (THAT IS
CHRIST) "IS COMING. WHEN HE COMES HE WILL TELL US EVERY-
THING." 26. JESUS SAID, "I AM HE, I WHO AM SPEAKING TO YOU NOW."

27. AT THAT MOMENT HIS DISCIPLES RETURNED, AND WERE ASTON-
ISHED TO FIND HIM TALKING WITH A WOMAN; BUT NONE OF THEM
SAID, "WHAT DO YOU WANT?" OR, "WHY ARE YOU TALKING WITH
HER?" 28. THE WOMAN PUT DOWN HER WATER-JAR AND WENT AWAY
TO THE TOWN, WHERE SHE SAID TO THE PEOPLE, 29. "COME AND SEE
A MAN WHO HAS TOLD ME EVERYTHING I EVER DID. COULD THIS BE
THE MESSIAH?" 30. THEY CAME OUT OF THE TOWN AND MADE THEIR
WAY TOWARDS HIM.

III.

3.1. THERE WAS ONE OF THE PHARISEES NAMED NICODEMUS, A
MEMBER OF THE JEWISH COUNCIL, WHO CAME TO JESUS BY NIGHT.
2. "RABBI," HE SAID, "WE KNOW THAT YOU ARE A TEACHER SENT BY
GOD; NO ONE COULD PERFORM THESE SIGNS OF YOURS UNLESS GOD

WERE WITH HIM." 3. JESUS ANSWERED, "IN TRUTH, IN VERY TRUTH I TELL YOU, UNLESS A MAN HAS BEEN BORN FROM ABOVE[4] HE CANNOT SEE THE KINGDOM OF GOD." 4. "BUT HOW IS IT POSSIBLE," SAID NICODEMUS, "FOR A MAN TO BE BORN WHEN HE IS OLD? CAN HE ENTER HIS MOTHER'S WOMB A SECOND TIME AND BE BORN?" 5. JESUS ANSWERED, "IN TRUTH I TELL YOU, NO ONE CAN ENTER THE KINGDOM OF GOD WITHOUT BEING BORN FROM WATER AND SPIRIT. 6. FLESH CAN GIVE BIRTH ONLY TO FLESH; IT IS SPIRIT THAT GIVES BIRTH TO SPIRIT. 7. YOU OUGHT NOT TO BE ASTONISHED, THEN, WHEN I TELL YOU THAT YOU MUST BE BORN FROM ABOVE. 8. THE WIND BLOWS WHERE IT WILLS; YOU HEAR THE SOUND OF IT, BUT YOU DO NOT KNOW WHERE IT COMES FROM, OR WHERE IT IS GOING. SO WITH EVERYONE WHO IS BORN FROM SPIRIT."

9. NICODEMUS REPLIED, "HOW IS THIS POSSIBLE?" 10. "WHAT!" SAID JESUS. "IS THIS FAMOUS TEACHER OF ISRAEL IGNORANT OF SUCH THINGS? 11. IN VERY TRUTH I TELL YOU, WE SPEAK OF WHAT WE KNOW, AND TESTIFY TO WHAT WE HAVE SEEN, AND YET YOU ALL REJECT OUR TESTIMONY. 12. *If you disbelieve me when I talk to you about things on earth, how are you to believe if I should talk about the things of heaven?*

13. *"No one ever went up into heaven except the one who came down from heaven, the Son of man whose home is in heaven.* 14. *This Son of man must be lifted up as the serpent was lifted up by Moses in the wilderness, so that everyone who has faith in him may in him possess eternal life.*

16. *"God loved the world so much that he gave his only Son, that everyone who has faith in him may not die but have eternal life.* 17. *It was not to judge the world that God sent his Son into the world, but that through him the world might be saved.*

18. *"The man who puts his faith in him does not come under judgment; but the unbeliever has already been judged in that he has not given his allegiance to God's only Son.* 19. *Here lies the test: the light has come into the world, but men preferred dark-*

ness to light because their deeds were evil. 20. *Bad men all hate the light and avoid it, for fear their practices should be shown up.* 21. *The honest man comes to the light so that it may be clearly seen that God is in all he does."*

The break between S and John probably occurs during 3.11 when Jesus switches from you singular to you plural. But there are two other possibilities. First, in Verse 11, Jesus may use you plural as "you, Nicodemus, and all like you," going on to the abstract you plural in verse 12. Then verse 12 would mark the beginning of the break. Second, the break occurs at the very beginning of verse 11, and John first keeps Jesus addressing Nicodemus.

IV.

7.45. The temple police came back to the chief priests and Pharisees, who asked, "Why have you not brought him?" 46. "No man," they answered, "ever spoke as this man speaks." 47. The Pharisees retorted, "Have you too been misled? 48. Is there a single one of our rulers who has believed in him, or of the Pharisees? 49. AS FOR THIS RABBLE, WHICH CARES NOTHING FOR THE LAW, A CURSE IS ON THEM." 50. THEN ONE OF THEIR NUMBER, NICODEMUS (THE MAN WHO HAD ONCE VISITED JESUS), INTERVENED. 51. "DOES OUR LAW," HE ASKED THEM, "PERMIT US TO PASS JUDGMENT ON A MAN UNLESS WE HAVE FIRST GIVEN HIM A HEARING AND LEARNED THE FACTS?" 52. "Are you a Galilean, too?" they retorted. "Study the scriptures and you will find that prophets do not come from Galilee."

I have attributed only verses 50 and 51 to S, and left the rest unattributed. Perhaps more comes from S. If only verses 50 and 51 were inserted from S by John, his aim was to use S to highlight the hypocrisy of the other Pharisees. In the original context they were to portray the good Nicodemus as a contrast to Jesus.

V.

19.38. After that, Pilate was approached by Joseph of Arimathea, a disciple of Jesus, but a secret disciple for fear of the Jews, who asked to be allowed to remove the body of Jesus. Pilate gave the permission; so Joseph came and took the body away. 39. HE WAS JOINED BY NICODEMUS (THE MAN WHO HAD FIRST VISITED JESUS BY NIGHT), WHO BROUGHT WITH HIM A MIXTURE OF MYRRH AND ALOES, MORE THAN HALF A HUNDREDWEIGHT. 40. THEY TOOK THE BODY OF JESUS AND WRAPPED IT, WITH THE SPICES, IN STRIPS OF LINEN CLOTH ACCORDING TO JEWISH BURIAL-CUSTOMS.

VI.

11.45. Now many of the Jews who had come to visit Mary and had seen what Jesus did, put their faith in him. 46. BUT SOME OF THEM WENT OFF TO THE PHARISEES AND REPORTED WHAT HE HAD DONE.

47. THEREUPON THE CHIEF PRIESTS AND THE PHARISEES CONVENED A MEETING OF THE COUNCIL. "WHAT ACTION ARE WE TAKING?" THEY SAID. "THIS MAN IS PERFORMING MANY SIGNS. 48. IF WE LEAVE HIM ALONE LIKE THIS THE WHOLE POPULACE WILL BELIEVE IN HIM. THEN THE ROMANS WILL COME AND SWEEP AWAY OUR TEMPLE AND OUR NATION." [PHARISEES OPPOSED SURRENDERING JESUS.] 49. BUT one of them, CAIAPHAS, *who was high priest that year,* SAID, 50. "YOU KNOW NOTHING WHATEVER; YOU DO NOT USE YOUR JUDGMENT; IT IS MORE TO YOUR INTEREST THAT ONE MAN SHOULD DIE FOR THE PEOPLE, THAN THAT THE WHOLE NATION SHOULD BE DESTROYED." 51. *He did not say this of his own accord, but as the high priest in office that year, he was prophesying that Jesus would die for the*

nation— 52. *would die not for the nation alone but to gather together the scattered children of God.* 53. *So from that day on they
plotted his death.*

I have not printed the account of the miracle itself. I believe the
account is basically an amalgam of S and of the redactor.

"Who was high priest that year" and "in office that year"
cannot be S. It may derive from another source of John, but is
most likely an unhelpful gloss of the redactor himself. It should
be stressed that, irrespective of any belief in S, something clearly
has disappeared from between the end of verse 48 and the beginning of 49.

VII.

2.13. As it was near the time of the Jewish Passover, Jesus went
up to Jerusalem. 14. THERE HE FOUND IN THE TEMPLE THE DEALERS
IN CATTLE, SHEEP, AND PIGEONS, AND THE MONEY-CHANGERS
SEATED AT THEIR TABLES. 15. JESUS MADE A WHIP OF CORDS AND
DROVE THEM OUT OF THE TEMPLE, SHEEP, CATTLE, AND ALL. HE
UPSET THE TABLES OF THE MONEY-CHANGERS, SCATTERING THEIR
COINS. 16. THEN HE TURNED ON THE DEALERS IN PIGEONS: "TAKE
THEM OUT," HE SAID; "YOU MUST NOT TURN MY FATHER'S HOUSE
INTO A MARKET." 17. *His disciples recalled the words of Scripture,
"Zeal for the house will destroy me."* 18. THE JEWS CHALLENGED
JESUS: "WHAT SIGN," THEY ASKED, "CAN YOU SHOW AS AUTHORITY
FOR YOUR ACTION?" 19. *"Destroy this temple,"* Jesus replied, *"and
in three days I will raise it again."* 20. *They said, "It has taken
forty-six years to build this temple. Are you going to raise it
again in three days?" But the temple he was speaking of was his
body.* 21. *After his resurrection his disciples recalled what he had
said,* 22. *and they believed the Scripture and the words that Jesus
had spoken.*

VIII.

5.1. Later on Jesus went up to Jerusalem for one of the Jewish festivals. 2. NOW AT THE SHEEP-POOL IN JERUSALEM THERE IS A PLACE WITH FIVE COLONNADES. ITS NAME IN THE LANGUAGE OF THE JEWS IS BETHESDA. 3. IN THESE COLONNADES THERE LAY A CROWD OF SICK PEOPLE, BLIND, LAME, AND PARALYZED. 5. AMONG THEM WAS A MAN WHO HAD BEEN CRIPPLED FOR THIRTY-EIGHT YEARS. 6. WHEN JESUS SAW HIM LYING THERE AND WAS AWARE THAT HE HAD BEEN ILL A LONG TIME, HE ASKED HIM, "DO YOU WANT TO RECOVER?" 7. "SIR," HE REPLIED, "I HAVE NO ONE TO PUT ME IN THE POOL WHEN THE WATER IS DISTURBED, BUT WHILE I AM MOVING, SOMEONE ELSE IS IN THE POOL BEFORE ME." 8. JESUS ANSWERED, "RISE TO YOUR FEET, TAKE UP YOUR BED AND WALK." 9. THE MAN RECOVERED INSTANTLY, TOOK UP HIS STRETCHER, AND BEGAN TO WALK.

10. THAT DAY WAS A SABBATH. SO THE JEWS SAID TO THE MAN WHO HAD BEEN CURED, "IT IS THE SABBATH. 11. YOU ARE NOT ALLOWED TO CARRY YOUR BED ON THE SABBATH." HE ANSWERED, "THE MAN WHO CURED ME SAID, 'TAKE UP YOUR BED AND WALK.'" 12. THEY ASKED HIM, "WHO IS THE MAN WHO TOLD YOU TO TAKE UP YOUR BED AND WALK?" 13. BUT THE CRIPPLE WHO HAD BEEN CURED DID NOT KNOW; FOR THE PLACE WAS CROWDED AND JESUS HAD SLIPPED AWAY. 14. A LITTLE LATER JESUS FOUND HIM IN THE TEMPLE AND SAID TO HIM, "NOW THAT YOU ARE WELL AGAIN, LEAVE YOUR SINFUL WAYS, OR YOU MAY SUFFER SOMETHING WORSE." 15. THE MAN WENT AWAY AND TOLD THE JEWS THAT IT WAS JESUS WHO HAD CURED HIM.

16. IT WAS WORKS OF THIS KIND DONE ON THE SABBATH THAT STIRRED THE JEWS TO PERSECUTE JESUS. 17. HE DEFENDED HIMSELF BY SAYING, "MY FATHER HAS NEVER YET CEASED HIS WORK, AND I AM WORKING, TOO." 18. THIS MADE THE JEWS STILL MORE DETERMINED TO KILL HIM, BECAUSE HE WAS NOT ONLY BREAKING THE SABBATH, BUT, [DENYING THE SABBATH] by calling God his own Father, he claimed equality with God.

19. To this charge Jesus replied, "In truth, in very truth I tell you, the Son can do nothing by himself; he does only what he sees the Father doing: what the Father does, the Son does. 20. For the Father loves the Son and shows him all his works, and will show greater yet, to fill you with wonder. 21. As the Father raises the dead and gives them life, so the Son gives life to men, as he determines. 22. And again, the Father does not judge anyone, but has given full jurisdiction to the Son; 23. it is his will that all should pay the same honor to the Son as the Father. To deny honor to the Son is to deny it to the Father who sent him."

I have left unattributed the end of verse 18. Jesus calling God his father could have been in S, and blasphemy (if this is blasphemy)—as well as the denial of the Sabbath—could have been charged against him. But equally, the thrust of S might simply have been the denial of the Sabbath, and John might have deflected it by introducing the accusation of blasphemy. I attribute verses 19 and 20 to John, but the stress on Jesus' working on the Sabbath and not on calling God his father is a reminiscence of S in verse 18 and in what I believe was deleted.

IX.

19.12. FROM THAT MOMENT PILATE TRIED HARD TO RELEASE HIM; BUT THE JEWS KEPT SHOUTING, "IF YOU LET THIS MAN GO, YOU ARE NO FRIEND TO CAESAR; 13. ANY MAN WHO CLAIMS TO BE KING IS DEFYING CAESAR." WHEN PILATE HEARD WHAT THEY WERE SAYING, HE BROUGHT JESUS OUT AND TOOK HIS SEAT ON THE TRIBUNAL AT THE PLACE KNOWN AS THE "THE PAVEMENT" ("GABBATHA" IN THE LANGUAGE OF THE JEWS). 14. IT WAS THE EVE OF PASSOVER, ABOUT NOON. PILATE SAID TO THE JEWS, "HERE IS YOUR KING." 15. THEY SHOUTED, "AWAY WITH HIM! AWAY WITH HIM! CRUCIFY HIM!" "CRUCIFY YOUR

S

KING?" SAID PILATE. "WE HAVE NO KING BUT CAESAR," THE JEWS RE-
PLIED. THEN AT LAST, TO SATISFY THEM, HE HANDED JESUS OVER TO BE
CRUCIFIED.

X.

19.31. BECAUSE IT WAS THE EVE OF PASSOVER, THE JEWS WERE ANX-
IOUS THAT THE BODIES SHOULD NOT REMAIN ON THE CROSS FOR THE
COMING SABBATH, SINCE THAT SABBATH WAS A DAY OF GREAT
SOLEMNITY; SO THEY REQUESTED PILATE TO HAVE THE LEGS BROKEN
AND THE BODIES TAKEN DOWN. (JESUS' LEGS WERE BROKEN.) 32. *The
soldiers accordingly came to the first of his fellow-victims and to
the second, and broke their legs; 33. but when they came to Jesus,
they found that he was already dead, so they did not break his
legs. 34. But one of the soldiers stabbed his side with a lance, and
at once there was a flow of blood and water. 35. This is vouched
for by an eyewitness, whose evidence is to be trusted. He knows
that he speaks the truth, so that you too may believe; 36. for this
happened in fulfillment of the text of Scripture: "No bone of his
shall be broken." 37. And another text says, "They shall look on
him whom they pierced."*

Verse 31 belongs to S because it specified that the Crucifixion occurred before the Passover.

When the relevant texts are set out in order, with different typefaces to denote different sources, it emerges that the work of
compilation was extremely simple for John, at least with regard to
S. It also emerges that in the accounts of action S was a very powerful source. I would suspect that S may have been used in other
episodes, but its presence is not apparent. Its strength must be revealing for the nature of John's audience.

17

EPILOGUE ON COMPOSITE SOURCES

✠ ✠ ✠

FOR READERS UNUSED TO FORM CRITICISM as applied to composite works, it may be instructive to look at two Roman law texts from Justinian's *Digest*, as they are viewed by modern scholars. The main point I want to make is that the history of these texts is thought to be much more complex than that I have suggested for S and the other source or sources used for episodes in John.

The first text is the definition of *furtum*, "theft," which was viewed as a civil wrong rather than a crime. The second concerns a particular problem in theft.

> Digest 47.2.1.3 (Paul, *book 39 on the Edict*) Furtum est contrectatio rei fraudulosa lucri faciendi gratia vel ipsius rei vel etiam usus eius possessionsive, quod lege natuali prohibitum est admittere.

> Theft is the fradulent handling of a thing for the sake of making a gain whether of the thing itself or even of its use or possession, which it is forbidden by the law of nature to commit.

The text is attributed to Paul, who was one of the most prominent jurists of the early third century.[1] The issue for modern scholars is to determine not only the substantive meaning but also how much of the definition genuinely comes from the pen of Paul, how much is due to Justinian's Byzantine compilers, and how much is the work of lawyers in between.[2] A first question arises because unusually we have a second definition attributed to Paul in *Pauli Sententiae* 2.31.1. Of course, whether that work itself is properly to be attributed to Paul has long been a matter for discussion.[3]

> Fur est qui dolo malo rem alienam contrectat.
>
> A thief is one who fraudulently handles wrongfully a thing belonging to another.

This definition omits mention of any intention to make a gain and speaks only of a thing, not also of its use or possession. Are these omissions significant for recovering the true thought of Paul? It also adds something not in the *Digest*, that the thing stolen belongs to another. But what if one, without permission, took from a creditor something he had given in pawn?

The *Digest* definition has *contrectatio*, "a wrongful handling or touching," and the genuineness of this word is not challenged. In all other contexts *contrectatio* involves a physical contact that somehow is wrongful, improper, or disgusting. But some legal texts seem to declare behavior as theft when the object has not been touched. Accordingly, some scholars would treat *contrectatio* here as meaning something wider, such as "meddling."[4]

Fraudulosa, "fraudulent," occurs only in this text and its parallel text in Justinian's elementary textbook for students, *Institutes*, 4.1.1. Also the correct formation of an adjective from *fraus*, "fraud," should give us *fraudulenta*. So the word is thought to be an interpolation, probably by the Byzantine compilers whose native language was Greek. Again, it is suggested that the word was not needed because *contrectatio* itself means that the handling was wrongful. Still, it might be that *fraudulosa* was more specific and indicates the nature of the wrong: after all, it corresponds to *dolo malo* in the definition in *Paul's Sentences.*

Lucri faciendi gratia, "for the sake of making a gain," are words that do not appear in the parallel text in the *Institutes* that otherwise gives Paul's *Digest* definition. Nor do they have a counterpart in the definition in *Paul's Sentences.* There are also texts that say there is theft, and yet an intention to make a gain is hard to find in them. Accordingly, *lucri faciendi gratia* is regarded as an addition to Paul's definition. But when was it added? By Justinian's compilers or before?

Vel ipsius rei vel etiam usus eius possessionisve, "whether of the thing or its use or its possession." Now we have a problem. If we delete *lucri faciendi gratia,* then theft is the wrongful handling of a thing, or its use, or its possession. But one cannot handle the use or possession of something. Unless we revert to holding that *contrectatio* need not involve touching, we must hold that these words are also a later addition to Paul.

At one level the simple solution would seem to be this. Paul's definition originally read: *Furtum est rei contrectatio,* "Theft is the wrongful handling of a thing." A jurist noticed that there could be theft of possession or use, so he added a marginal gloss in his manuscript to "thing": "of the thing itself, its use, or possession." Later, a scribe, transcribing the manuscript, by mistake inserted the gloss into the text. The Byzantine compilers of the *Digest* noticed the ensuing illogicality and inserted *lucri faciendi gratia* to come up with "for the sake of making a gain of the thing: whether of the thing itself, its use, or possession." As usual, the draftsmen of the *Institutes* did not look at the work of their *Digest* colleagues,[5] failed to spot the illogicality, and so did not insert *lucri faciendi gratia.* So far, so good. But if the draftsmen of the *Digest* and of the *Institutes,* both involved in making a composite work from earlier sources, did not work together, bang goes the theory that the wrongly formed *fraudulenta* is a Byzantine insertion. Both sets of draftsmen could not have come up with the idea that the same element was missing from the definition, and both have invented the same impossible word.

The second text, which concerns a particular situation, had its origin in Ulpian's book 37 on the *Edict* and is now *Digest* 47.2.52.20

Si quis asinum meum coegisset et in equas suas τῆς γονῆς dumtaxat χάριν admisisset, furti non tenetur, nisi furandi quoque animum habuit. Quod et Herennio Modestino studioso meo de Dalmatia consulenti rescripsi circa equos quibus eiusdem rei gratia subiecisse quis equas suas proponebatur, furti ita demum teneri si furandi animo id fecisset, si minus, in factum agendum.

If someone drove off my stallion ass, and turned him in among his own mares only for breeding purposes, he is not liable for theft unless he also had the intention to steal. I also wrote this to my student, Herennius Modestinus, who consulted me from Dalmatia. The facts involved stallions that a man was supposed to have turned in among his mares for the same purpose. I replied he was liable for theft only if he acted with the intention of stealing; if not, an *actio in factum* (action on the facts) should be brought.

The text is notorious, quite properly. The use of the ass has been appropriated, quite improperly. This seems a clear case of theft. Why, for Ulpian, should there be an extra requirement that the wrongdoer (for such he is in Ulpian's opinion or he would not allow an action on the facts) *also* have an intention to steal? What is this extra intention, anyway? For many scholars, moreover, there is a further problem: for them, only the subjective Byzantines, not also the objective Roman jurists, could have laid such stress on intention.[6] Accordingly, the history of the text is much controverted. The solutions are as numerous as the demons that entered the Gadarene swine.[7]

The tasks in using the available sources that faced the compilers of the *Digest* and the redactor of John were different, and I am not claiming otherwise. My claims are, first, that both were tied to earlier sources, from which they could not escape. Second, in combining earlier sources, or the old and the new, inconsistencies, inelegances, and peculiarities result which become apparent to critical, trained scholars. Third, to someone versed in Roman law scholarship, the role suggested for John in using S and at least one earlier source has nothing strange in it. And, finally, the actual work of amalgamating S with other sources, as presented here, was not one of great difficulty.

Most serious New Testament scholars do not dispute that John was dependent on various preexisting sources. When the issue is put, these scholars cannot deny the strong possibility that sources that had to be dealt with presented conflicting views. The argument of many is, of course, that the sources cannot now be separated out, given the absence of independent material.[8] One of my points is that, except in one regard,[9] the task of distinguishing the sources of John is simpler than that faced every day by Roman law scholars in determining the amount of interference in classical legal texts by subsequent hands. The extent of disagreement among modern Roman lawyers indicates the difficulty of the task, not its impossibility. In both cases, the methodology is the same: texts must be examined for inconsistencies of all kinds inside a text and between one text and another. In John I have found, I believe, glaring inconsistencies with his overall message, inconsistencies that point to a source of a particular kind. I have tried to pinpoint the episodes where that source most clearly appears. Nothing else. I have not attempted the difficult task of identifying all of John's sources or of identifying different christological levels.

In chapter 7 I inserted a quotation from Raymond E. Brown's *Community of the Beloved Disciple* on the perils of reconstructing John's sources. It is fitting to end on the note that the reconstruction of S involves far simpler problems than does his own reconstruction of the history of the Johannine community.

✟

ABBREVIATIONS

✟   ✟   ✟

Ashton, *Understanding*	John Ashton, *Understanding the Fourth Gospel* (Oxford, 1991).
Barrett, *St. John*	C. K. Barrett, *The Gospel according to St. John*, 2d ed. (Philadelphia, 1978).
Brodie, *Gospel*	Thomas L. Brodie, *The Gospel according to John* (New York, 1993).
Brown, *Community*	Raymond E. Brown, *The Community of the Beloved Disciple* (New York, 1979).
Brown, *John I–XII*	Raymond E. Brown, *The Gospel according to John: I–XII* (Anchor Bible, New York, 1966).
Brown, *John XIII–XXI*	Raymond E. Brown, *The Gospel according to John: XIII–XXI* (Anchor Bible, New York, 1970).
Bultman, *John: A Commentary*	Rudolf Karl Bultmann, *The Gospel of John: A Commentary* (Philadelphia, 1971).
Crossan, *Historical Jesus*	John D. Crossan, *The Historical Jesus* (San Francisco, 1991).
Culpepper, *Anatomy*	R. Alan Culpepper, *Anatomy of the Fourth Gospel* (Philadelphia, 1983).

Daube,
New Testament

David Daube, *The New Testament and Rabbinic Judaism* (London, 1956).

Davies,
Invitation

William David Davies, *Invitation to the New Testament* (Garden City, N.Y., 1966).

Davies,
Rhetoric

Margaret Davies, *Rhetoric and Reference in the Fourth Gospel* (Sheffield, 1992).

Derrett,
Law

J. Duncan Derrett, *Law in the New Testament* (London, 1970).

Dodd,
Tradition

C. H. Dodd, *Historical Tradition in the Fourth Gospel* (Cambridge, 1965).

Fox,
Unauthorized Version

Robin Lane Fox, *The Unauthorized Version: Truth and Fiction in the Bible* (New York, 1992).

Gossip,
Bible, 8

A. J. Gossip, in the *The Interpreter's Bible*, 8 (New York, 1952).

Grant,
Historical Introduction

Robert M. Grant, *A Historical Introduction to the New Testament* (London, 1963).

Howard
Bible, 8

W. F. Howard, in *The Interpreter's Bible*, 8 (New York, 1952).

Hull,
Commentary, 9

W. E. Hull, in *The Broadman Bible Commentary*, 9 (Nashville, 1970).

Painter,
Quest

John Painter, *The Quest for the Messiah*, 2d ed. (Nashville, 1993).

Schnackenburg,
Gospel, 1, 2

Rudolf Schnackenburg, *The Gospel according to St. John*, 1, 2 (New York, 1980).

Schürer,
Jewish People, 2

Emil Schürer, *The History of the Jewish People in the Age of Jesus Christ (175 B.C.– A.D. 135)*, 2, 2d ed., eds. Geza Vermes, Fergus Millar, Matthew Black, Martin Goodmar, and Pamela Vermes (Edinburgh, 1986).

Strack-Billerbeck,
Kommentar, 1, 2

Herman L. Strack and Paul Billerbeck, *Kommentar zum Neuen Testament aus Talmud und Midrasch*, 1, 5th ed. (Munich, 1969); 2, 4th ed. (Munich, 1965).

Zeitlin,
Jesus

Irving M. Zeitlin, *Jesus and the Judaism of His Time* (Cambridge, 1988).

NOTES

✠ ✠ ✠

Introduction

1. I have kept references to modern works to a minimum. In general I cite others only when they add point to my argument whether I am in agreement or disagreement with them. For bibliography, see now Ashton, *Understanding*; Brodie, *Gospel*; Thomas L. Brodie, *The Quest for the Origin of John's Gospel* (New York, 1993).

2. Alan Watson, "Jesus and the Woman of Samaria," *International Journal of Moral and Social Studies* 8 (1993): 179ff.

3. Bultmann postulated (at least) two preexisting sources for John, a miracle source and a source of revelation discourses: *John: A Commentary*, pp. 6f. In the former he also sees additions of the evangelist that are clearly separable. The limits of this second source, he believes, cannot be defined with certainty.

His postulated sources and mine do not coincide, though there is overlap, particularly with his miracle source. The overlap, in my view, has nothing to do with a miracle source but with the overall subject matter of the source that I have tried to isolate and that I have designated "S".

4. Fox, *Unauthorized Version*, p. 139.

5. See, for example, Arland D. Jacobson, *The First Gospel: An Introduction to Q* (Sonoma, Calif., 1992), and the works he discusses; cf. John D. Crossan, *Jesus: A Revolutionary Biography* (San Francisco, 1994).

Chapter 1. Form Criticism

1. See, for example, Denys L. Page, *Folktales in Homer's Odyssey* (Cambridge, Mass., 1973).

2. See, for example, Gerhard von Rad, *Genesis: A Commentary*, trans. J. H. Marks (Philadelphia, 1961), pp. 23ff.

3. See, for example, Davies, *Invitation*, pp. 81, 90ff., 97ff., 382ff.; Grant, *Historical Introduction*, pp. 59ff.; Davies, *Rhetoric*, pp. 255ff.; Brevard S. Childs, *The New Testament as Canon: An Introduction* (Philadelphia, 1984), pp. 131ff.

4. *C. de novo codice componendo*, § 2; cf. Alan Watson, "Prolegomena to Establishing Pre-Justinianic Texts," *Tijdschrift voor Rechtsgeschiedenis* 62 (1993), pp. 113ff at p. 115.

5. *C. Deo auctore*, § 9.

6. See now Watson, "Prolegomena."

7. See Alan Watson, *Contract of Mandate in Roman Law* (Oxford, 1961), pp. 36ff.

8. See, for example, Grant, *Historical Introduction*, pp. 284ff. For recent attempts to reconstruct the life of Jesus see, for example, John D. Crossan, *Historical Jesus*, and the authors he cites, pp. xxvii f.

9. Hence, apart even from other arguments, the obvious absurdity of attempts (such as that of Tony Honoré, *Ulpian* [Oxford, 1982]) to plot the chronology of Ulpian's writings from unusual linguistic usage and construction.

10. John 13.23; 19.26; 20.2; 21.7, 20, 24; cf. Davies, *Invitation*, pp. 377ff.

11. See, for example, Grant, *Historical Introduction*, pp. 117ff. More and more the relationship between the Synoptic Gospels is questioned: see, for example, H. Riley, *The Making of Mark: An Exploration* (Macon, Ga., 1989).

12. Grant, *Historical Introduction*, p. 154.

13. Ibid.; see also Brown, *John I–XII*, pp. xlivff.; Davies, *Invitation*, pp. 382ff.; Schnackenburg, *Gospel*, 1, pp. 26ff.; D. Moody Smith, *Johannine Christianity* (Columbia, S.C., 1984), pp. 97ff., 145ff.; but see also my chapter 13.

Chapter 2. Introductory Matters

1. See, for example, Brown, *John I–XII*, pp. xxivff.; Davies, *Invitation*, pp. 382ff.; U. C. von Wahlde, *The Earliest Version of John's Gospel* (Wil-

mington, Del., 1989). A convenient summary of the rearrangement suggested by Bultmann is in Grant, *Historical Introduction*, pp. 160ff.

2. It is, of course, not my claim that John used only one narrative source, the one that I term "S." But to avoid the charge that I act arbitrarily in assigning some episodes to S, but not others that might seem contrary to my claim, I will examine and emphasize, and assign to S, *all* the episodes that appear only in John, and the major part of *all* the episodes that are in the Synoptics and John, but where John's account is significantly different.

3. Brown, *Community*, p. 17.

4. For impossible inconsistencies in the Synoptic Gospels for events surrounding the birth of Jesus see, for example, Fox, *Unauthorized Version*, pp. 27ff.

5. *Oxford Classical Dictionary*, 2d ed., s.v. "Tacitus, Cornelius."

6. For hostility to Christians under Nero see also Suetonius, *Nero*, 16.2.

7. *Oxford Classical Dictionary*, 2d ed., s.v. "Suetonius Paulinus, Gaius."

8. For the correct interpretation of these letters see above all, G. E. M. de Ste. Croix, "Why Were the Early Christians Persecuted?" *Past and Present* 26 (1963): 6ff.; "Why Were the Early Christians Persecuted?—an Amendment," *Past and Present* 27 (1964): 23ff.; see also Robin Lane Fox, *Pagans and Christians* (London, 1986), p. 749.

9. *Oxford Classical Dictionary*, 2d ed., s.v. "Josephus, Flavius."

10. *Contra Celsum*, § 1.47; *Commentarius in Matthaeum*, 13.55.

11. *Historia Ecclesiastica*, 1.11; *Demonstratio Evangelica*, 3.5.105.

12. See, for example, Louis H. Feldman, *Josephus*, 9 (Cambridge, Mass., 1965), p. 49 n. b; Zeitlin, *Jesus*, 139ff.

13. Grant believes it to be highly unlikely that any authentic original version can be reached: *Historical Introduction*, p. 292. Fox claims that the whole passage "is agreed to be a Christian addition": *Unauthorized Version*, p. 284.

14. See, for example, Feldman, *Josephus*, 9, p. 49 n. b; Davies, *Invitation*, p. 65; Crossan, *Historical Jesus*, p. 373.

15. Cf. Geza Vermes, *Jesus and the World of Judaism* (London, 1983), pp. 6ff.

16. Suetonius, *Divus Vespasianus*, 7; Tacitus, *Historiae*, 4.81; Dio Cassius, 65.8.

Chapter 3. The Wedding Feast at Cana

1. Ashton, *Understanding*, pp. 266f.

2. Brown says that Johannine notices of time sometimes have significance, sometimes not: *John I–XII*, p. 75. But the example he gives for a lack of significance is noon in 4.6, and in chapter 4 I will argue that noon there is very significant.

3. Brown, *John I–XII*, pp. 97f.

4. Judges 14.12; Tobit 11.19.

5. See, for example, Brown, *John I–XII*, p. 98.

6. Ashton, *Understanding*, p. 268. Possibly the invitation to Jesus and the disciples came through Nathaniel, who was from Cana; cf. Painter, *Quest*, p. 189.

7. For example, Ashton, *Understanding*, p. 268. For Schnackenburg, this is not clear: *Gospel*, 1, p. 327.

8. J. Duncan Derrett, *Law in the New Testament* (London, 1970), pp. 228ff.

9. Dodd, *Tradition*, p. 226.

10. See, for example, Schnackenburg, *Gospel*, 1, p. 328.

11. Matthew 15.28; Luke 13.12; John 4.21, 8.10, 20.13.

12. Brown, *John I–XII*, p. 99; see also Strack-Billerbeck, *Kommentar*, 2, p. 401.

13. Judges 11.12; 2 Chronicles 35.21; 1 Kings 17.18.

14. 2 Kings 3.13; Hosea 14.8.

15. J.-P. Michaud, "Le Signe de Cana dans son contexte Johannique," *Laval Théologique et Philosophique* 19 (1963): 257ff., at pp. 267f; cf. Painter, *Quest*, pp. 189ff.

16. Cf. Barrett, *St. John*, p. 191.

17. Pace C. Goodwin, one cannot argue that John 2.4 is a quotation of Zaraphath in a very different and amazing context: "How Did John Treat His Sources?" *Journal of Biblical Literature* 73 (1954): 61ff., at p. 63. That approach would demand that Matthew and Mark also quoted Zaraphath in amazing contexts. Goodwin uses only arguments of this kind to show John's use of sources; accordingly, his view must be discounted.

18. On Semitisms in New Testament Greek, see, for example, Daube, *New Testament*, pp. 102ff.

19. In the present state of our knowledge it is as impossible to judge the accuracy of quotations in the four canonical Gospels as it is to decide whether Peter and Jesus expressed the sentiments attributed to them in the Gospel of Thomas, Saying 114: "Simon Peter said to them, 'Let Mary leave us, for women are not worthy of life.' Jesus said, 'I myself shall lead her in order to make her male so that she too may become a living spirit resembling you males. For every woman who will make herself male will enter the kingdom of heaven.'" Cf. Fox, *Unauthorized Version*, pp. 149f.

20. Brown, *John I–XII*, p. 100.

21. For wine as an integral part of Jewish feasts see Strack-Billerbeck, *Kommentar*, 2, pp. 400f.

22. See, above all, David Daube, "Wine in the Bible" (St. Paul's Lecture, London, 1974).

23. Genesis 9.21–22.

24. Genesis 19.32–36.

25. Lavishness is noted by Schnackenburg, *Gospel*, 1, p. 332.

26. Schnackenburg refers to it as a village wedding: ibid., p. 323.

27. For rebuttal of suggestions that the water turned into wine was not that in the jars, but in a well, or only that drawn off from the jars, see Brown, *John I–XII*, p. 100. These suggestions derive from discomfort at the great quantity of water turned into wine; cf. Barrett, *St. John*, p. 192. Brodie notices the enormous quantity of water turned into wine, but for him this provides "a delightful surprise": *Gospel*, p. 171.

28. Cf. Strack-Billerbeck, *Kommentar*, 2, pp. 405ff.

29. Leviticus 11.33–35; Mishnah Kelim 2.3.

30. See Mishnah Berakhot 8.2; Mishnah Hagigah 2.5; Babylonian Talmud, Hagigah 18b (no need to wash for fruit); Babylonian Talmud, Hullin 106a.

31. Brown, *John I–XII*, p. 100.

32. Ibid., p. 101.

33. Schnackenburg notes that the story breaks off "rather suddenly": *Gospel*, 1, p. 343. That the steward (at 2:10) praises the bridegroom for his generosity is no indication that all or even many of the guests felt the same way.

34. Daube, *New Testament*, pp. 44f.

35. See, for example, Euripides, *Bacchae*, 704ff.; Athenaeus, *Learned Banquet*, 1.34a; Pausanias, *Description of Greece*, 6.261f.

36. Barrett, *St. John*, p. 188.

37. Derrett, *New Testament*, p. ix.

38. Marcel Mauss, *The Gift, Forms, and Functions of Exchange in Archaic Societies*, trans. I. Cunnison (London, 1954).

39. Derrett, *New Testament*, pp. 228ff.

40. Ibid., p. 233 n. 3.

41. Pace Derrett, "Jesus and his disciples had received an unlimited invitation. He provided an almost unlimited supply of wine at the feast": ibid., p. 243. If I am correct in supposing that Jesus had five disciples with him—see chapter 4—then for each invitation Jesus responded with around 150 bottles.

Chapter 4. The Samaritan Woman

1. Genesis 24.11; see also Hull, *Commentary*, 9, p. 250; Howard, *Bible*, 8, p. 521; Gossip, *Bible*, 8, p. 521.

2. See, for example, Strack-Billerbeck, *Kommentar*, 2, pp. 431f.; Barrett, *St. John*, p. 231.

3. Marcus Dods, in *The Expositor's Greek Testament*, 1, ed. W. Robertson Nicoll (Grand Rapids, 1974). Cf. Howard, *Bible*, 8, p. 521; Painter, *Quest*, p. 200.

4. A parallel request is that of Abraham's servant to Rebecca in Genesis 24.17–20.

5. A translation such as that of *The New English Bible* is inaccurate: "Jews and Samaritans, it should be noted, do not use vessels in common." Only the Jews were exclusive, and that is expressed in the Greek.

6. I am not persuaded by David Daube's suggestion (in an otherwise convincing paper) that she was expressing surprise at his kindness in being willing to drink from her vessel: "Jesus and the Samaritan Woman: the Meaning of συγχράομαι" *Journal of Biblical Literature* 69 (1950): 137ff.

7. For this as the meaning of συγχράομαι see Daube, "Jesus and the Samaritan Woman"; cf. Barrett, *St. John*, p. 232.

8. See, for example, Brown, *John I–XII*, p. 325; Davies, *Invitation*, p. 33.

9. Strack-Billerbeck, *Kommentar*, 2, p. 436.

10. John 4.6.

11. Schnackenburg's treatment is revealing: *Gospel*, 1, p. 428. For him, the "woman is moved by Jesus's words but has not grasped their profounder meaning. Hearing Jesus's offer of 'living water' she misunderstands it as a promise of something earthly and natural. . . . She is interested in the 'living water' but can only think of the water in the well of Jacob. Still, she now addresses the stranger respectfully as 'sir,' and asks him 'whence' he can procure this water without a vessel to draw it in."

12. Ashton, *Understanding*, p. 190; cf. p. 219.

13. See Strack-Billerbeck, *Kommentar*, 2, p. 437.

14. In the *Broadman Bible Commentary*, 9, p. 24.

15. (New York, 1966), p. 939 n. c. Sexual symbolism is, of course, extremely common. For examples from Latin, see J. N. Adams, *The Latin Sexual Vocabulary* (Baltimore, 1982), pp. 82ff.; for visual examples from Dutch painting, see Simon Schama, *The Embarrassment of Riches* (Berkeley, 1982), pp. 433f., 473f.

16. See, for example, Jean M. Auel, *The Plains of Passage* (New York, 1990), p. 59.

17. Calum Carmichael also notices the sexual overtones in the episode, but he gives the whole encounter a spiritual meaning: "Marriage and the Samaritan Woman," *New Testament Studies* 26 (1979): 332ff.: also see my chapter 7.

18. See, for example, Strack-Billerbeck, *Kommentar*, 2, p. 437; Hull, *Commentary*, 9, p. 250; Gossip, *Bible*, 8, pp. 521f. Gossip also suggests that she "was a trachled, futile creature always behindtime."

19. The heat of noon is the time of rest and also of dalliance: cf. Song of Songs 1.7.

20. See, for example, Genesis 38. 13–21.

21. Cf. Schnackenburg, *Gospel*, 1, p. 424.

22. See, for example, Howard, *Bible*, 8, p. 520.

23. Brown, *John I–XII*, p. 169.

24. In *The Class Struggle in the Ancient Greek World* (Ithaca, N.Y., 1981), p. 428, de Ste. Croix describes Sychar as "a mere village, of course." He has in mind, I believe, the English notion of a village—not all that tiny.

25. See, for example, *The Biblical World*, ed. Charles F. Pfeiffer (Grand Rapids, 1966), p. 522.

26. Daube, "Jesus and the Samaritan Woman," p. 137; cf. Painter, *Quest*, p. 199.

27. Mishnah Niddah 4.1. A.D. 65 or 66 is the date supported by Daube. The regulation was certainly before the destruction of the Temple in 70: Babylonian Talmud, Shabbath 13b, 16b. The date is quite uncertain, but it is after the division of the schools of Shammai and Hillel: cf. I. Epstein, *Babylonian Talmud: Seder Móed*, 1 (London, 1938), p. 54 n. 1.

28. It should be noted that, though he does not say so, Daube's treatment of the woman leaving her pot behind presupposes a source such as I am suggesting. The realistic detail has a real meaning and direct relevance to the story, yet it has nothing to do with John's theological message.

29. Of course, the significance of the detail is not just that the woman left her pot behind but that John treats the detail as worth recording. For Schnackenburg there is no need to see anything in the detail except that she wants to return home quickly and unimpeded: *Gospel*, 1, p. 443.

30. But at 13.29 some disciples thought Jesus was sending Judas by himself to buy food for thirteen.

31. Schnackenburg, *Gospel*, 1, p. 424.

32. The significance of the disciples' absence is not noted, for instance, by Bultmann, *John: A Commentary*, Barrett, *St. John*, or Brown, *John I–XII*, though Bultmann (p. 178) and Barrett (p. 231) stress that it was natural for Jesus to be tired at that time of day. Barrett calls the removal of the disciples "a stage direction," and some scholars see 4.8 as an insertion by John into the episode. But if it were natural for Jesus to be tired, why not also the disciples?

Chapter 5. Nicodemus

1. See, for example, the short treatment in Davies, *Rhetoric*, pp. 336f.; Culpepper, *Anatomy*, pp. 134ff.

2. See, for example, Strack-Billerbeck, *Kommentar*, 2, pp. 412f.

3. Brown, *John I–XII*, pp. 129f.

4. Hull in *Commentary*, 9, p. 239.

5. Brown prefers a symbolic interpretation: Nicodemus was coming out of the dark (evil) into the light (good): *John I–XII*, p. 130. A third sug-

gestion is that it may reflect the rabbinic custom of studying late at night: see, for example, Strack-Billerbeck, *Kommentar*, 2, pp. 419f.; Schnackenburg, *Gospel*, 1, pp. 365f.

6. For Barrett, "Nicodemus appears before Jesus but never even states the purpose of his coming": *St. John*, p. 202. He is not given the chance!

7. Brown, *John I–XII*, p. 138. Hull finds the discontinuity between Nicodemus's remarks and Jesus' response "startling": *Commentary* 9, p. 240.

8. See Brown, *John I–XII*, p. 130; Strack-Billerbeck, *Kommentar*, 2, pp. 420ff.

9. For Culpepper, the misunderstanding reveals Nicodemus's limitations: *Anatomy*, p. 135.

10. Bultmann, *John: A Commentary*, p. 144.

11. Cf. Brown, *John I–XII*, p. 131.

12. There is a pun on the Greek πνευμα (3.7f.), which means both "wind" and "spirit." But the pun could equally have been on the Hebrew and Aramaic *ruah*.

13. Bultmann, *John*, p. 144.

14. In private correspondence David Daube injects a note of caution with a reference to his paper "Judas," *California Law Review* 82 (1994), pp. 95ff. In that paper he observes that Judas's betrayal of Jesus led in Matthew to his self-punishment by hanging (27.3ff.), in Acts to punishment from above: he fell headlong, he burst open in the middle, and all his bowels gushed out (1.16ff.). He relates the more savage punishment in Acts to the time of its production: Christians were more secure and demanded more of the faithful. Likewise in John, for Daube Jesus was demanding a great deal from those interested in his message.

15. 2 Chronicles 16.14.

16. "The Silver Blaze," in Doyle, *The Memoirs of Sherlock Holmes* (New York, 1892).

17. Mishnah Oholoth 1.

18. See also Numbers 19.16, 31.19.

19. The reason for defilement for entering the praetorium is the subject of much debate: see, for example, Brown, *John XIII–XXI*, p. 846.

20. Numbers 9.6ff.

21. An explanation for the resurrected Jesus not appearing to Lazarus is given in chapter 7.

22. But, pace the Authorized Version, he is not described as coming at night, a fact that once made me doubt the source of the episode.

23. The more usual translation in the form of a question does not quite fit the negative in the sentence.

24. Cf. Mark 3.22; Geza Vermes, *Jesus and the World of Judaism*, pp. 4f.; 11f.

25. Reference is also sometimes made to Josephus, *Jewish War* 1.209; Josephus, *Jewish Antiquities* 14.107; Septuagint, Dan Sus 51.

26. Severino Pancaro, *The Law in the Fourth Gospel* (Leiden, 1975), pp. 138ff. Pancaro also gives full citation to modern literature. Treatment of John 7.51 by modern scholars is very unsatisfactory.

27. For Gossip, "Nicodemus was a great soul, possessed of enviable qualities, and bursting through difficulties to which most of us would have tamely surrendered": *Bible*, 8, p. 503.

Chapter 6. The Raising of Lazarus

1. For a modern account see above all E. Mary Smallwood, *The Jews under Roman Rule* (Leiden, 1976), passim.

2. Matthew 27.15f., 38; Mark 15.6f., 27; Luke 23.18f., 32f.; John 18.39f., 19.18.

3. See, for example, Schürer, *Jewish People*, 2, pp. 488ff.

4. Brown, *John I–XII*, p. 429.

5. Ibid., pp. 428ff. Brown's whole treatment of the subject is excellent.

6. For Barrett, 11.45–54 "no doubt comes from John's pen": *St. John*, p. 404.

7. See, for example, Schürer, *Jewish People*, 2, pp. 212f.

8. Brown, *John I–XII*, p. 439.

9. Cf. Howard, *Bible*, 8, p. 651; Barrett, *St. John*, p. 406.

10. The Greek λησταί brigands, (Matthew 27.38; Mark 15.27) is a term used by Josephus to designate those who took up arms against the Romans; *Jewish War* 2.228, 2.253, 2.254, 2.271, 4.198; *Jewish Antiquities* 20.161.

11. Cf., for example, Smallwood, *Jews*, p. 164.

12. *Jewish Antiquities* 18.116–19.

13. Matthew 3.11f.; Mark 1.7f.; Luke 3.15–17; John 1.19–27.

14. See, for example, Davies, *Invitation*, pp. 391f.

15. Numbers 35.25ff.

16. See, for example, Bultmann, *John*, p. 410 n. 10. Brown's attempt to surmount the difficulty is weak and not to the point: *John I–XII*, pp. 439f.

17. I am not excluding the possibility of some overlap between the sources. Caiaphas could have appeared in both.

18. Cf. J. Wellhausen, *Erweiterungen und Änderungen im vierten Evangelium* (Berlin, 1907), p. 26; Brown, *John I–XII*, p. 431; Ernst Bammel, *"Ex illa itaque die consilium fecerunt . . . ."* in *The Trial of Jesus*, ed. Ernst Bammel (Naperville, Ill., 1970, pp. 11ff. at pp. 12, 14f.

Chapter 7. The Four Episodes

1. Calum Carmichael, "Marriage and the Samaritan Woman," *New Testament Studies* 26 (1979): 332ff., at p. 335.

2. I find Calum Carmichael's similar arguments about the Decalogue persuasive: *The Origins of Biblical Law* (Ithaca, N.Y., 1992), pp. 22ff. I am grateful to Carmichael for letting me read three chapters of his forthcoming book, *Narratives of Creation*. The chapters discuss the wedding feast at Cana, Jesus' meeting with the Samaritan woman, and the first intervention of Nicodemus.

3. In private correspondence David Daube tells me: "I always assumed the realistic background that you postulate."

4. But for Gossip, Caiaphas's words are "malevolent": *Bible*, 8, 651.

5. *Collaboration with Tyranny in Rabbinic Law* (Oxford, 1965); now reprinted in *Collected Works of David Daube, I, Talmudic Law*, ed. Calum Carmichael (Berkeley, 1992), pp. 63ff. Daube takes the matter further and deals with Caiaphas in *Appeasement or Resistance* (Berkeley, 1987), pp. 75ff. The whole treatment brings out the horrible dimensions of the dilemma.

6. One might refer here to Mishnah Berakhot 9.5 (end), which has traditionally been interpreted to mean that in exceptional circumstances a law may be set aside to preserve the whole system of law.

7. Josephus, *Jewish Antiquities*, 18.35.

8. Daube, *Appeasement or Resistance*, pp. 86f.

9. Like Daube, I am passing no moral judgment on collaboration.

10. See, for example, Fox, *Unauthorized Version*, pp. 15ff., especially at p. 23.

Chapter 8. S and the Synoptic Gospels

1. Matthew 27.57; Mark 15.42ff.; Luke 23.50ff.; John 19.38ff.
2. John 18.10f.
3. Matthew 26.69ff.; Mark 14.66ff.; Luke 22.54ff.
4. Mark 10.35ff.
5. Matthew 20.24; Mark 10.41ff.
6. The episode of the cleansing of the Temple will be discussed in chapter 9.
7. See, for example, I. Howard Marshall, *The Gospel of Luke* (Grand Rapids, 1978), pp. 490ff.
8. For them see Wolfgang Kunkel, *Herkunft und soziale Stellung der römischen Juristen*, 2d ed. (Graz, 1967), pp. 12, 18.
9. For other views of the Scaevolae relating to law and religious observance see Cicero, *De legibus*, 2.19.47ff.
10. Exodus 16.23ff., 20.8ff., 23.12, 31.12ff., 34.21, 35.1ff.; Leviticus 23.3; Numbers 15.32ff.; Deuteronomy 5.12ff. See also Isaiah 58.13; Jeremiah 17.21ff.; Ezekiel 22.8; Amos 8.5; Nehemiah 10.32, 13.15ff.
11. See, for example, *The Mishnah*, trans. Herbert Danby (Oxford, 1933), pp. xxf.
12. On the question of whether Jesus violates the law by working on the Sabbath see, above all, Severino Pancaro, *Law in the Fourth Gospel*, pp. 9ff.
13. Matthew 12.1f.; Mark 2.23f.; Luke 6.1f. For the revolutionary nature of Jesus' behavior, see Daube, *New Testament*, p. 182.
14. On this see Daube, *New Testament*, pp. 67ff.
15. See, for example, B. Schaller in *Der Kleine Pauly*, 4 (Munich, 1975), pp. 772ff.
16. *Life of Moses*, 2.4.22.
17. Curing the withered hand: Matthew 12.9ff.; Mark 3.1ff.; Luke 6.6ff.; woman with infirmity of spirit: Luke 13.10ff.; man with dropsy, Luke 14.1ff. In John 5.2ff., telling the paralytic to carry his pallet is an apparent breach of the Sabbath.

18. See the extensive citations in Strack-Billerbeck, *Kommentar*, 1, pp. 622ff.

19. But see Zeitlin, *Jesus*, pp. 74ff.

20. Dodd, *Tradition*, p. 231.

21. It may be suggested that the delay increases the effectiveness of Jesus' message. Yes, but Jesus is shown to be hostile to giving signs. Brodie remarks, "The crisis of Lazarus's sickness is all the more dramatic because Jesus' response to it seems so measured": *Gospel*, p. 383.

22. Whether or not his conduct amounted to the crime of blasphemy I need not here consider: in John he is never accused of that crime.

Chapter 9. *John and the Synoptic Gospels*

1. See, for example, D. Daube, "Some Reflections on the Historicity of the New Testament," *Catholic Commission on Intellectual and Cultural Affairs Annual* (1980): 1ff., at pp. 4f.

2. See, for example, Brown, *John I–XII*, pp. 116ff.

3. Matthew 17.27. For the temple dues see Mishnah Shekalim.

4. It is noticeable that Jesus deals differently with the dove sellers.

5. See Mishnah Zebahim.

6. See, for example, Deuteronomy 17.1.

7. Cf. Strack-Billerbeck, *Kommentar*, 1, p. 850.

8. See Broadie, *Gospel*, p. 179.

9. Barrett, *St. John*, p. 197.

10. W. E. Hull, *Commentary*, 9, p. 235.

11. Brown, *John I–XII*, p. 115.

12. See, for example, Barrett, *St. John*, p. 197.

13. On the translation and theological meaning see Brown, *John XIII–XXI*, pp. 549f.

14. Ibid., p. 556.

15. *The Eucharistic Words of Jesus*, 3d ed., trans. Norman Perrin (New York, 1966), pp. 41ff.; cf. Harold Riley, *The Making of Mark: An Exploration* (Macon, Ga., 1989), pp. 228ff.

16. See, for example, Julius Wellhausen, *Das Evangelium Johannis* (Berlin, 1908), p. 60; Joachim Jeremias, *Eucharistic Words*, p. 82.

17. Jeremias, *Eucharistic Words*, p. 49.

18. Jerusalem Talmud, Pesahim 10.1.37b: "R. Levi has said 'because slaves eat standing, here [at the Passover meal] people should recline to eat, to signify that they have passed from slavery to freedom.'" R. Levi was active around 300.

19. See, for example, Mark 14.3; Luke 7.36f., 49; 11.37; 14.15. For many other references see Jeremias, *Eucharistic Words*, p. 48.

20. Jeremias, *Eucharistic Words*, p. 49. Mishnah Pesahim 10.1; Tosefta Pesahim 10.1; the translation of the former text is inaccurate in Herbert Danby, *Mishnah*, p. 150. The treatment by Barrett, *St. John*, p. 441, of washing is informative and useful, but he seems to miss the point of religious purity. Brown is skeptical of Jeremias's claim that the disciples were levitically pure: *John XIII–XXI*, p. 567.

21. If my overall argument is correct, and S shows Jesus as hostile to Jewish ritual, then 13.10 (and presumably the surrounding verses) does not derive from S.

22. Matthew 26.26; Mark 14.22; Luke 22.19.

23. David Daube, *He that Cometh* (St. Paul's Lecture, London, 1966), pp. 6ff., quotation from p. 13. Daube had a forerunner in Robert Eisler, "Das letzte Abendmahl," *Zeitschrift für die Neutestamentliche Wissenschaft* 24 (1925): 161ff. Cf. D. B. Carmichael, "David Daube on the Eucharist and the Passover Seder," *Journal for the Study of the New Testament* 42 (1991): 45ff.

24. But Euccharistic-like details appear in John 6.50–58. Their presence, as we shall see, is very awkward.

25. For Fox it is John who has the timing right: *Unauthorized Version*, pp. 294f. His main argument seems to be that "it rests on a primary source": cf. his pp. 204ff.

26. *Encyclopedia Judaica*, 13 (Jerusalem, 1971), s.v. Passover.

27. Cf. Dodd, *Historical Tradition*, pp. 96ff.

28. Cf. the discussions in Barrett, *St. John*, pp. 543f., and Fox, *Unauthorized Version*, pp. 298f. Though he writes from a very different perspective, Fox's whole account of the arrest and trial of Jesus in John is excellent. We need not decide whether by this time "friend of Caesar" was a technical term.

29. Philo, *Embassy to Gaius*, 299ff.; Josephus, *Jewish Antiquities*, 18.55ff., 85ff.; *Jewish War*, 2.169ff.

30. Though my primary concern is with the existence of a tradition rather than with the historical accuracy of the tradition, I wish to put on

record my lack of belief in the custom attributed to Pilate of releasing to the Jews one prisoner chosen by them; cf. Paul Winter, *On the Trial of Jesus* (Berlin, 1961), pp. 91ff. In the troubled Judaea under Roman occupation such a policy was just unreasonable. Also, it seems out of keeping with what we know otherwise about Pilate's relations with the Jews. I would suggest a different scenario. Pilate, who did not regard Jesus as messianic, certainly did not want to put Jesus to death, and he proposed to release him. But the crowd, whether incited by the Pharisees or disillusioned by Jesus' failure to live up to expectations as the Messiah, or both, demanded his death. Still with the same objective, Pilate made an offer he thought the crowd could not refuse. He would release one prisoner with the crowd having a choice. He expected them to choose Jesus because of their recent enthusiasm. But they insisted on Bar Abbas. The tradition used by the evangelists was uninterested in Jewish relations with the Romans, and the once-off event came to be seen as a custom. For this lack of interest, see, for example, Fox, *Unauthorized Version*, pp. 27ff.

But the custom, if it existed, was particular to Pilate: it is so described in the Gospels and does not appear otherwise whether in Judaea or in any other Roman province. But the possibility that it existed for Pilate raises a serious issue for this book and for the nature of early Christianity, an issue that cannot be resolved. The question is, at what point of time did Pilate offer to release a prisoner, shortly before or shortly after Passover? One automatically assumes just before. The reprieve would add to the festivities. But there are strong arguments to the contrary. Just before Passover, the Jews might well request the release of a revolutionary (perhaps captured after great Roman effort). After all, what joy would the release of an ordinary thief or murderer give the generality? And since Passover would be the time of greatest political tension and possible rioting, Pilate could scarcely risk releasing an obvious troublemaker. To habitually release a prisoner just after Passover could seem to provide Pilate with some guarantee of good behavior from the masses. For the masses, a release just after Passover had the advantage of increasing the choice: three days' worth of victims would be available, not just one; those whose execution would not be complete before Passover, those arrested on Passover (when no execution would take place), and those arrested just after.

The issue is crucial, because if any such release occurred before Passover, then John's account of the Last Supper and the Crucifixion could be close to historical reality, and the accounts in the Synoptics could not.

31. It would be a mistake to suggest that in John the involvement of the Jewish authorities in Jesus' death is the work of the redactor and not of S.

32. See, for example, Haim Cohen, *The Trial and Death of Jesus* (New York, 1971), pp. 94ff.

33. Daube, *New Testament*, pp. 303ff.

Chapter 10. S, John, and the Four Episodes

1. But see the closing paragraphs of chapter 14. See also, most recently, Thomas L. Brodie, *Quest for the Origin of John's Gospel*.

2. Cf., for example, Alan Watson, *Roman Law and Comparative Law* (Athens, Ga., 1991), pp. 182ff.

3. On Bultmann—in the original German version—see D. Moody Smith, *The Composition and Order of the Fourth Gospel* (New Haven, 1965). See also Ashton, *Understanding*, pp. 3ff.

4. Brown, *John I–XII*, p. 103.

5. Contrast Matthew 10.5.

6. Cf. Schnackenburg, *Gospel*, 2, p. 324.

7. See also John 20.30.

8. See Davies, *Invitation*, pp. 391ff.

9. On the confusion see, for example, Bultmann, *John*, pp. 641ff.; Brown, *John XII–XXI*, pp. 828ff.

10. Pace Davies, *Invitation*, p. 391. The error, failing to treat John as a composite, is easy to make.

11. See already Emil Schürer, *Vorträge der theologischen Konferenz zu Giessen* (Giessen, 1889), p. 68.

12. Barrett, *St. John*, p. 406; cf. Brodie, *Gospel*, p. 399.

13. For the purposes of this book it does not matter whether the redactor of John was or was not Jewish.

14. Particularly useful for knowledge of Jewish matters in John is Fox, *Unauthorized Version*, pp. 206ff. He writes from a different perspective and oddly considers John a primary source, not a composite work.

Chapter 11. The Paralytic at the Pool

1. See the extensive citations in Strack-Billerbeck, *Kommentar*, 1, pp. 622ff.

2. See, for example, Immanuel Jakobovits, *Jewish Medical Ethics* (New York, 1959), pp. 74ff.

3. Mishnah Shabbath, especially 7.2: cf. Strack-Billerbeck, *Kommentar*, 2, pp. 454ff. Rabbi Jose even went so far as to prohibit a cripple going out wearing his wooden leg: Mishnah Shabbath 6.8.

4. Cf. Zeitlin, *Jesus*, p. 67.

5. But the sources are mainly later: cf. Strack-Billerbeck, *Kommentar*, 2, pp. 461ff. See also Brown, *John I–XII*, pp. 216f.

6. Philo, *Allegorical Interpretation of Genesis* 2.5.

7. See, for example, Bultmann, *John*, p. 244; Barrett, *St. John*, p. 256ff.

8. For the famous *crux* of μαλλον, see, for example, Ashton, *Understanding*, pp. 517f.

Chapter 12. "He Who Saw This"

1. For a discussion of problems arising from the grammatical structure, see Brown, *John XII–XXI*, pp. 936f.

2. For a synopsis of views on Peter and bibliography see P. A. Mirecki, in *The Anchor Bible Dictionary*, 5 (New York, 1992), pp. 278ff. He is not always accurate; for example, he writes that the legs broken were those of Jesus, and this does not seem a viable translation. See also Fox, *Unauthorized Version*, p. 148.

3. This is the translation of C. Maurer, in Edgar Hennecke, *New Testament Apocrypha*, 1, ed. Wilhelm Schneemelcher (Philadelphia, 1963), p. 184.

4. P. Gardner-Smith, "The Gospel of Peter," *Journal of Theological Studies* 27 (1926): 255ff., at p. 256.

5. J. D. Crossan, *The Cross That Spoke* (San Francisco, 1988), pp. 16ff.

6. See, for example, Brown, *John XIII–XXI*, pp. 937f.

7. Further supposed links—Jesus as the lamblike Suffering Servant, or his being represented as a Passover victim—do little to provide evidence that Jesus was identified as the paschal lamb: pace, for example, J. R. Miles in *The Anchor Bible Dictionary*, 4 (New York, 1992), p. 133.

8. Indeed, to conceive of Jesus, the Lamb of God, as the paschal lamb is no easy feat.

9. See, for example, the writers referred to by Brown, *John XIII–XXI*, pp. 937f.

10. An enormous amount has been written on the factuality and theological significance of blood and water coming out of Jesus' side (19.34): see, for example, Brown, *John XIII–XXI*, pp. 946ff.; Barrett, *St. John*, pp. 556f.

Chapter 13. The Subject of S

1. Bultmann, *John: A Commentary*, p. 189 n. 6.

2. Brown, *John I–XII*, p. 172.

3. That the Samaritans may have had a different idea than the Jews about a "Messiah" is irrelevant. But see Brown, *Community*, p. 44.

4. Galatians 2 makes it probable that Matthew 10.5f. gives correctly the view of Jesus; cf., for example, Zeitlin, *Jesus*, pp. 49f. But it should be noted that in Luke 17.12ff., of the ten lepers cured by Jesus, the one who praised God was a Samaritan.

5. Still, the episode is much more pointed in John than it is in the Synoptics: see Daube, *New Testament*, pp. 40ff.

6. Two of these episodes appear rather different from the others, with more significant detail, and must somehow have importance in the development of John. These are the healing of the official's son (4.46ff.) and making the blind man see (9.1ff.). I cannot categorize the first as being from S, and in chapter 14 I treat the second as not being from S. An excellent introduction to both episodes will be found in Barrett, *St. John*, pp. 244ff. and pp. 353ff. I would add Jesus' washing the disciples' feet (13.3ff.): for me this is fully explained by Daube, *New Testament*, pp. 182ff.

7. I am, of course, not suggesting that at times, in the Synoptic Gospels untouched by S and in John from sources other than S, Jesus is not sometimes portrayed as hostile to the law. He is: see, for example, Matthew 12.1ff., 12.9ff.; Mark 2.23ff., 3.1ff.; John 9.1ff.

Chapter 14. S and Not S

1. Cf. Schnackenburg, *Gospel*, 2, pp. 247f.

2. See, for example, Barrett, *St. John*, 356; Brown, *John I–XII*, p. 371. In 5.14, however, Jesus' words imply that sin is the cause of sickness.

3. Cf., for example, Brown, *John I–XII*, p. 375.

4. On the extent of any expulsion, see, for example, Barrett, *St. John*, pp. 361f.

Chapter 15. Conclusions

1. See, for example, Zeitlin, *Jesus*, p. 54.

2. Brown, *Community*. See especially his chart on pp. 166f.

3. Cf. Brown, *Community*, p. 41; Edward Geoffrey Parrinder, *Son of Joseph: The Parentage of Jesus* (Edinburgh, 1992), p. 51. For Parrinder, the picture of all the Jews as opposed to Jesus comes from the evangelist and is inflammatory. It is the view of John, I believe, but it was, for a different purpose, already set out in S.

4. See, for example, most recently, Fox, *Unauthorized Version*, pp. 207ff. For W. H. Brownlee, the Gospel of John was put together by a disciple from manuscripts left by John the Apostle, and the author of the Gospel as we have it translated from the Aramaic whatever needed translating: "Whence the Gospel according to John?" in *John and the Dead Sea Scrolls*, ed. James H. Charlesworth (New York, 1990), pp. 166ff. A sophisticated discussion of authorship is in Schnackenburg, *Gospel*, 1, pp. 75ff.

5. It is just much simpler to notice that the arguments that seem to favor Fox's thesis are adequately explained by the hypothesis of S.

6. Though I believe he exaggerates, Calum Carmichael is right in spotting links between episodes: "Marriage and the Samaritan Woman," *New Testament Studies* 26 (1979): 332ff. Thus, Jesus' first discourse on being born from above through water and spirit is linked with John the Baptist's discussion on baptism and spirit, which is linked with "living water" and the woman's belief in Jesus at Jacob's well.

7. I would like to call attention to a further difference between the Synoptics and John: in the Synoptics Jesus is represented as both a law breaker and a law maker, in John in this context Jesus appears only as a law breaker. It would take us too far from my main theme to examine the matter in full, but a few points may be apposite. Thus, in the Synoptics, the treatment of restricting divorce is not presented as resulting from any dubious behavior of Jesus, and his position is supported by legalistic reasoning (Matthew 5.31f.; 19.3ff.; Mark 10.2ff.; Luke 16.18). The topic is not dealt with in John. Likewise, Jesus' declaration in the Synoptics that no

food is forbidden does not proceed from any behavior of his and is justified by reasons (Matthew 15.10ff.; Mark 7.14ff.). Again, the subject does not appear in John. With regard to Sabbath prohibitions Jesus in the Synoptics goes further in defending the behavior of his disciples in plucking grain by very legal reasoning (Matthew 12.1ff.; Mark 2.23ff.) than he does in any context in John. (On this subject see Daube, *New Testament*, pp. 67ff.)

Chapter 16. S

1. The use made of very small quotations from the Old Testament—see chapter 3 n. 16—is not evidence for how he approached traditions about Jesus: contra, C. Goodwin, "How did John treat his sources?" *Journal of Biblical Literature* 73 (1954): 61ff. John's treatment of one set of sources—background material—provides no argument for his treatment of the sources that provided the incentive and the challenge. Besides, there is the very real problem of knowing the authority and text of what we now regard as the books of the Old Testament: see, for example, Fox, *Unauthorized Version*, pp. 114ff.

2. See, for example, Fox, *Unauthorized Version*, p. 246.

3. *The New English Bible* has "mother," but that is an interpretation, not an acceptable translation.

4. *The New English Bible* has "over again."

Chapter 17. Epilogue on Composite Sources

1. See, for example, Wolfgang Kunkel, *Herkunft und soziale Stellung der römischen Juristen*, 2d ed. (Graz, 1967), pp. 244f.

2. Because this chapter is meant to be illustrative only, references will be kept to a minimum. For what follows on the definition, see, for example, Alan Watson, "The Definition of *Furtum* and the Trichotomy," in *Studies in Roman Private Law* (London, 1991), pp. 269ff.

3. See, for example, Ernst Levy, *Pauli Sententiae* (Ithaca, 1945).

4. This is certainly not my view, but it was passionately defended by J. A. C. Thomas. After his death I kept his translation as "interference," in *Digest of Justinian*, 4, ed. Theodor Mommsen, Paul Krueger, and Alan Watson (Philadelphia, 1985), p. 737.

5. Cf. Justinian's *Institutes*, 3.23. pr; 4.6.7; 4.9pr.

6. Instructive is H. F. Jolowicz, *Digest XLVII.2: De Furtis* (Cambridge, 1940), pp. lviii, 76.

7. For my solution see Alan Watson, "*D* 47.2.52.20: the Jackass, the Mares and *Furtum*," in *Studies*, pp. 305ff.

8. Still, in evaluating John, there is no excuse for forgetting that it is a composite work.

9. That regard is that the original author of each *Digest* text is identified.

✠

INDEX OF TEXTS

✠ ✠ ✠

I. OLD TESTAMENT

INDEX

2. NEW TESTAMENT

3. RABBINIC SOURCES

4. CLASSICAL SOURCES